DATE DUE

WITHDRAWN

Standardizing English

TENNESSEE STUDIES IN LITERATURE VOLUME 31

Standardizing English

Essays in the History of Language Change

IN HONOR OF JOHN HURT FISHER

Edited by Joseph B. Trahern, Jr.

The University of Tennessee Press
KNOXVILLE

TENNESSEE STUDIES IN LITERATURE

Editorial Board: Allison R. Ensor, Thomas J. Heffernan, B.J. Leggett, Norman Sanders, Jon Manchip White

"Tennessee Studies in Literature," a distinguished series sponsored by the Department of English at The University of Tennessee, Knoxville, began publication in 1956. Beginning in 1984, with Volume 27, TSL evolved from a series of annual volumes of miscellaneous essays to a series of occasional volumes, each one dealing with a specific theme, period, or genre, for which the editor of that volume has invited contributions from leading scholars in the field.

Inquiries concerning this series should be addressed to the Editorial Board, Tennessee Studies in Literature, Department of English, The University of Tennessee, Knoxville, Tennessee 37996-0430. Those desiring to purchase additional copies of this issue or copies of back issues should address The University of Tennessee Press, 293 Communications Building, Knoxville, Tennessee 37996-0325.

Publication of this book has been aided by a grant from The Better English Fund, established by John C. Hodges at The University of Tennessee, Knoxville.

The paper in this book meets the minimum requirements of the American National Standard for Permanence of Paper for Printed Library Materials. ♾ The binding materials have been chosen for strength and durability.

Library of Congress Cataloging-in-Publication Data

Standardizing English : essays in the history of language change, in honor of John Hurt Fisher / edited by Joseph B. Trahern, Jr. — 1st ed.
    p. cm. — (Tennessee studies in literature ; v. 31)
    Includes bibliographies.
    ISBN 0-87049-600-x (cloth: alk. paper) :
    1. English language—Standardization. 2. English language—History.
I. Fisher, John H. II. Trahern, Joseph B., 1937– . III. Series.
PE1074.7.S74 1989
428—dc19   88-26029 CIP

Contents

Introduction

Joseph B. Trahern, Jr.

The essays in this volume address a wide variety of aspects of the English language: phonology, syntax, dialects, vocabulary, stylistics, and meter. The texts they investigate range from the Old English Laws through fourteenth-century poetry, Shakespeare's plays, the records of London Bridge, and translations of the Bible, up to recordings of speech in Texas. The essays represent a diversity of approaches and points of view, tied together by the attempt to illuminate a number of aspects of the tendency toward standardization of the language at various periods of its history. Each acknowledges, either directly or indirectly, the influence of the work on standard English which has been a major part of the scholarly effort of John Hurt Fisher. For some, the influence has been an idea to be tested in another linguistic area in another historical period; for others, Fisher's hypotheses have themselves been tested—sometimes reinforced and on occasion challenged. Each of these eight British and American linguists and literary historians has offered an essay which extends the limits of his or her own work in one of the several aspects of the study of standardization. It is hoped that their coming together to celebrate the important work of a respected colleague will not only provide a volume which offers both a unity of purpose and a variety of perspectives, but that it will also stimulate the reader to further exploration of a number of the areas of inquiry which so fortuitously benefit from the influence of John Fisher's work.

In "Elements of a Written Standard in the Old English Laws," Mary P. Richards, noting the lack of agreement as to what constituted Standard Old English, seeks to examine in the Anglo-Saxon period the types of materials examined by John Fisher in his discussion of Chancery Standard—"those produced for functional purposes by a staff assisting the king . . . for whatever light they may shed on the question of standardization. In the Anglo-Saxon period, these materials are the royal diplomas (in Latin), and legal codes, charters, wills, writs, and related documents (in Old English and Latin)." Noting that the Old English laws "provide a body of related materials issued by royal authority over five centuries, surviving in multiple copies, that should give evidence of standardizing tendencies in the language if such existed," Richards looks for such evidence through a review of the manuscript contexts in which the laws were preserved, the impact of the church on the language, structure, and style of the legal codes, and the evidence leading to the definition of the formal components of a written legal tradition. Richards is able to find a number of similarities among the codes she examines, but she notes changes as well, observing however that the changes occur within the general traditional framework of the laws so that the new codes remain clearly identifiable as part of the longer tradition. She also points out that variations in style appear so gradually that "older forms are not supplanted but decrease in frequency of occurrence." The evidence from the study of vocabulary indicates that there are certain preferences which occur from code to code and suggest that the authors were conscious of writing traditional materials that required a traditional vocabulary. She concludes that "the standardizing elements in the laws probably emerge from the environment in which they were written, for the effort to follow traditional models produced a high degree of uniformity in the materials, a uniformity worthy of the later office of Chancery."

In "Sources of Standardisation in Later Middle English," J. D. Burnley begins by noting that the phrase "Standard English" in modern times "denotes a form of language—that is of its phonology, morphology, syntax, and lexis—which is superordinate to geographically variant forms, and which is realised in both spoken and written modes, and in the latter by a consistent orthography." He points out, however, that Middle English standards differ sharply from this modern conception in two respects: they exist only in the written mode (since standardization in spoken English belongs to a later period), and "the consistency of their orthography does not approach that of Modern Standard English." Standardization, Burnley observes, has both "a linguistic descriptive dimension, having to do with the technique of representation in writing, and a sociolinguistic one concerned with the breadth of its use." Noting that in the case of Chancery Standard more attention has been paid to the former than to the latter, he seeks in his essay some evidence for a climate of opinion "propitious for the acceptance and extension of a standard in the broader sense, an intellectual and cultural disposition to match the mechanical extension of the orthography of Chancery." He first seeks evidence of a concern for consistency in the spelling of English, then turns to the evidence for the desirability of a standard form of written English, and finally he examines the motivations underlying the adoption of standard forms. These concerns lead Burnley to an examination of fifteenth-century manuscripts of Chaucer, observations on language by Roger Bacon, Osbern Bokenham, and others, and to the conclusion that "throughout the thirteenth and fourteenth centuries England did indeed possess a standard written language, but paradoxically that language was a form of French," and that the curial style characteristic of the documents produced in Chancery Standard influenced prose writers both in England and in France. From the English perspective in the fifteenth century, moreover, "this style derived further esteem by its association with French, the language of cultural prestige in medieval England." The association of this style with Chancery orthography, Burnley concludes, may have contributed to the extension "from the narrow register of its original use to the broader one of literary use."

Thomas Cable's contribution, "Standards from the Past: The Conservative Syllable Structure of the Alliterative Revival," offers evidence against the assertion in traditional grammars and handbooks that final -*e* was lost in the West Midlands at the end of the alliterative revival. Cable studies the final syllables of the words at the ends of the lines in *Cleanness* and offers conclusions which can be generalized to the ends of lines of other poems from the period. Cable's investigation involved a complete scansion and grammatical parsing of all 1,812 lines of *Cleanness*, as well as a notation of the etymology of every word and "a marking of every syllable that would have occurred historically—i.e., as the word would have appeared in Old English, Old French, Old Norse, or Latin." From this evidence Cable argues "that final *-e* was essential in fourteenth-century alliterative meter because the end of the first half-line allowed an unstressed syllable optionally, but the end of the second half-line had an unstressed syllable 99 percent of the time." He then sets forth a number of phonological rules for final *-e,* some of which, he notes, "flatly contradict the most familiar grammars, but only because the grammars do not take into account different registers." Finally, Cable uses the patterns which began to materialize in the final syllable at the end of each hemistich to reach conclusions about the other slots in the hemistich, noting that "the end of each half-line, in effect, cast a network of implicature leftward," and concluding that at the end of the first half-line "there can be one, or two, or no unstressed syllables," whereas "there must be exactly one unstressed syllable at the end of the long line." He notes that "more important than the specific rules of this essay . . . is the outline of a self-confirming method that will apply to some sixty thousand lines of fourteenth-century Middle English."

In "Standardising Shakespeare's Non-Standard Language," N. F. Blake notes that as the English language became more regulated, writers were able to exploit the differences between the standardized version of the language and other varieties. Since the other varieties were marked not by any internal consistency but by their difference from the standard, and since they progressively sank lower in esteem, no attempt was made to standardize them; but as they became associated with provincial or uneducated speakers, writers of literary works picked up aspects of them "to provide some colour and verisimilitude to their portrayal of character." Blake notes that these writers never attempted to provide a complete representation of the speech of such people but rather merely used the speech to indicate that a different, less prestigious variety of language was to be understood. From this perspective, Blake investigates two editorial problems involving what the author actually wrote in his attempt to represent non-standard language and what the modern editor, especially an editor who regularizes elsewhere, should do with it.

After a brief examination of Chaucer's *Reeve's Tale*, the first English literary text to attempt to exploit the difference between standard and non-standard varieties of English, Blake moves to an examination of three short speeches by Edgar from *King Lear* in a speech mode "used in contemporary plays for the peasant class in the south of England" as they occur in the 1608 Quarto, the First Folio, and in a modern edition, the Arden. Blake notes editorial additions both of standard and non-standard forms, but a clear tendency in each case toward regularization: unusual forms are altered in order to be more readily recognized, non-standard syntactic irregularities are smoothed out, but some readily recognizable dialectal forms or expressions are extended beyond the use of the earlier text.

Blake tests these findings against *King Henry IV, Part One*, and *Henry V* and finds a wealth of data leading to the conclusion that it is necessary "to distinguish two types of non-standard language: dialect speech and low-class language." Editors and compositors picked up more readily the distinctive features of the former and introduced them even more thoroughly into the speeches of the characters in question. The evidence in the latter category is less clear. Blake concludes by noting that while many modern editions opt for modern spelling, "which means standardising the text in accordance with modern conventions," there is no agreement on conventions for representing non-standard language. He offers the provocative suggestion that since modern editors follow the Folio in introducing more of the accepted conventions for non-standard speech than are found in the quartos, they might "carry the procedure to its logical conclusion [i.e., producing "standardized" dialectical forms] if their intention is to produce an edition with standardised spelling."

In "Chancery Standard and the Records of Old London Bridge," C. Paul Christianson tests John Fisher's case for a Chancery Standard against the records of the London Bridge trust, whose accounts run continuously through the period of supposed

Chancery influence. Christianson is able to identify ten Clerks of the Works who kept records continuously from 1381–82 until 1501–2; the documents they wrote fall into two main categories: muniments and annual accounts. The evidence points to a developing interest in Secretary script in the 1440s and 1450s, though it does not answer the question of the reason for its adoption— whether or not it was due to an increased use of Secretary among Chancery scribes prominent in the scribal community, as suggested by Fisher. Christianson goes on to examine complementary texts alongside the bridge records and "finds the consistent use of many preferred Chancery forms for English," concluding that the bridge records provide "circumstantial evidence that an awareness of Chancery practices on the part of the Bridge Clerks was a likely possibility."

In "The Standardization of English Relative Clauses," Michael Montgomery explores the evolution of relative clauses in English through an examination of more than sixteen hundred of them in four closely comparable written sources—English versions of the *Acts of the Apostles* from the fourteenth, seventeenth, nineteenth, and twentieth centuries. Montgomery codes the clauses according to "a system of ten groups of formal and functional factors," which permit a comparison in which nearly all variables are controlled. He is quick to point out some problem areas, however, such as the fact that each text translates from different combinations of original documents, the fact that any translator has personal idiosyncrasies which may not be typical of his day, and the fact that different translators may have had different ideas about the most appropriate style for a religious text. He notes, however, that the quantity of the data from each version should contribute to a minimizing of the distorted effects of these problems. Montgomery presents his evidence based on the ten factors in tabular form with extensive evaluative commentary and concludes that his analysis "only suggests the rich possibilities of studying subsystems of a language like relativization in order to describe the evolving structure of English." He does, however, offer a number of enlightening summary statements about the standardizing of relative clauses, conclusions which not only contribute to the larger study of standardization but offer clear insights into particular aspects of the evolution of relative clauses, which have heretofore been studied in only the most general terms.

In "Americanisms, Briticisms, and the Standard: an Essay at Definition," John Algeo observes that "all of us tend, as a practical matter, to think of the variety of the language we use as 'the' language and of other varieties as curious departures from the rational, simple, and esthetic norm represented by our own language habits." Noting that the term *English* is now itself ambiguous, Algeo proceeds to a fascinating historical discussion of the use of the suffix *-ism* to denote a feature belonging to a national standard of an international language, noting a number of ethnocentric biases and prejudicial implications in a variety of dictionaries. He examines seventy definitions for nationalisms, distributed among nineteen dictionaries, demonstrating substantial and enlightening differences in referential focus, in types of distinction, in geographical area of reference, and in standards of contrast. Algeo concludes convincingly that "most dictionaries need a more consistent definition schema for nationalism terms than they now have," but he warns that "we cannot decide what is to count as a variation belonging to a national variety until we have defined the metalanguage we use to talk about them." This essay is an excellent beginning in that direction.

Guy Bailey's essay, "Sociolinguistic Constraints on Language Change and the Evolution of *Are* in Early Modern English," begins with a discussion of a number of constraints on language change suggested by John Fisher in his work on the Chancery Standard and goes on to discuss the continuing operation of three of them in the evolution of the Black English Vernacular in the United States over the last seventy-five years. He notes that while these constraints illustrate some of the social mechanisms involved in language change, the linguistic mechanisms are less clear. "When two grammatical forms are of equal social prestige," he asks, "why (or perhaps how) is it that one displaces or comes to be preferred over another? After surveying the various plural forms of *to be* from the fifteenth through the eighteenth centuries and noting that not until the seventeenth century does any grammar give *are* as the only plural form *(be* remaining an alternative until the middle of the eighteenth century), Bailey notes that from the mid-eighteenth century on *be,* despite its early prominence and sanction in the grammars and usage guides, became restricted to regional dialects. It was replaced, curiously, by a form which had itself originally been restricted in the same way.

In the light of the historical background, Bailey examines the present tense of *be* in BEV through evidence derived from recordings of three groups of black informants: children born between 1972 and 1975, adults born between 1890 and 1930, and former slaves born between 1844 and 1864, all from one place in Texas. The evidence for the latter two groups is remarkably similar, but in the children there is a dramatic increase in the use of *be* (as opposed to *is/are* or the zero copula), which occurs more than four times as often as it does in the speech of the adults. Bailey goes on to note, however, that almost all of the examples of this increased use of *be* occur before present participles and that its occurrence elsewhere is quite similar in all three groups of informants. He sees this as a result of the linguistic process of reanalysis, produced by the creation of distinct black speech communities in a social context which allowed *be* to be reanalyzed as a marker of durative/habitual aspect while retaining zero-copula and the conjugated forms to signal progressive and future meanings. That said, Bailey goes back to speculate that the same principle may have motivated the replacement of *be* by *are* as a plural at an earlier stage in the development of English, concluding that the change from *be* to *are* "reflects a movement toward transparency, toward a more optimal code wherein each surface unit has a distinct, recognizable form."

Readers who have read this far have already noticed one editorial bias concerning standardization—the fact that the American editor, quoting a British contributor, allows the word *standardization* itself to stand with two different spellings in the same sentence. Nor has the spelling been nationalized in the various essays. Another bias in the same direction should be noted: while consistency in citation form has been achieved in most instances, three of the essays vary from the standard because in the editor's judgment alternate forms of citation contribute materially to the clarity of the contribution. This was a conscious decision for which the editor is fully responsible.

The volume opens with a tribute to John Fisher by Thomas Heffernan and closes with a bibliography of Professor Fisher's scholarly writings, compiled by Mark Allen and Judith Fisher. These contributions speak eloquently for themselves and need no editorial introduction.

For John Hurt Fisher

Thomas J. Heffernan

It is a singular pleasure for me to have been invited to summarize the career of John Hurt Fisher. Few of his generation have done so much to advance the cause of the humanities internationally. The essays in this volume are presented to him by colleagues on his retirement from the Department of English of the University of Tennessee.

My pleasure in briefly recounting John's quite extraordinary career is tempered by the knowledge that a half-century's service to higher education cannot be compassed in a few pages. Let these jottings serve then, as Augustine says in the *Confessions*, as a sign pointing to a larger world.

John Hurt Fisher was born in Lexington, Kentucky, in 1919, just as his parents were on the point of joining the Presbyterian Board of Foreign Missions as educational missionaries to Persia (as it was then called). He celebrated his first birthday in Bombay, India, and then traveled by rail to Calcutta, up the Persian Gulf to Basra, Iraq, and finally by horse and wagon to Hamadan (the ancient Etebana in the Book of Ruth). He lived for the next fourteen years in this ancient summer capital of Darius and Xerxes: Hamadan, Iran. John's youth was genuinely Kiplingesque: he was tutored by his parents in the classics in the mission compound, cared for by an Assyrian nurse and playing with Persian children. His early years were thus trilingual—Assyrian, Farsi, and English.

On his return to the States, John attended Maryville College and took his B.A. *cum laude* in 1940. At Maryville, although determined to study history, his favorite course turned out to be the History of English Language as taught from Albert Baugh's venerable *History of the English Language*. His choice to do his graduate work at the University of Pennsylvania was undoubtedly influenced by Professor Baugh's position on that faculty. While John was at Pennsylvania, his abiding interest in the classics, nurtured by his parents, turned toward the Middle Ages. The fruit of his study was his dissertation, an edition of *The Tretyse of Loue* under Baugh's direction, later published by the Early English Text Society.

John's forty-six years of uninterrupted teaching began at Pennsylvania in 1942, the same year in which he married his college sweetheart, partner, and collaborator for forty-five years, Jane Law Fisher. It is not my intent to give a chronological account of his distinguished career as scholar, teacher, administrator, and leader in higher education. The facts are available in pertinent reference books. However, I would be remiss if I did not share at least some of the high points of this virtually legendary career. After leaving Pennsylvania, John taught at New York University (1945–55), at Duke University (1955–60), at Indiana University (1960–62), at New York University again (1962–72), and at the University of Tennessee as the John C. Hodges Professor of English (1972–88). In addition, John taught summers or short periods at Yale, Michigan, and at the University of Southern California. Thousands of students, both undergraduate and graduate, have benefited from his generosity, his sense of humor, and his openness to different points of view.

Outside the classroom, John Fisher's contribution to higher education, and especially to the profession of language teaching, came through his many responsibilities in the Modern Language Association. John helped William Riley Parker organize the MLA Conference of 1948, and afterwards served as Assistant Secretary (1949–51), Treasurer (1952–55), Executive Secretary and Editor of the *Publications of the Modern Language Association* (1963–71), Vice-President (1972–73) and President 1974, the third President elected from the south in the organization's ninety-year history (two of them, J. Douglas Bruce and Fisher, medievalists from the University of Tennessee). What this summary of duties and dates does not reveal is the tremendous challenge John Fisher undertook in leading the foremost organization of its kind during its period of most rapid growth—the MLA grew from ten thousand to thirty-four thousand during his tenure. In 1979 John helped found the New Chaucer Society. He served as its President in 1982, and tirelessly as Executive Director since 1982. He is a Fellow of the Medieval Academy of America and served as its President in 1988. Surely *fortuna* was at work when it happened that the Medieval Academy meeting at which he presided as President in April 1988 was at his alma mater, the University of Pennsylvania.

Perhaps John's broad vision of the responsibility of the scholar-educator was a result of the *felix culpa* of his early years: a childhood and adolescence which saw very palpably the salutary effect of education on the Iranian young. If that is the case, then it is no less true that he has thrown himself tirelessly into those associations with which he has been involved. Surely a sign of their affection is the recognition these many distinguished bodies in turn have awarded him. John has served as a consultant to the United States Office of Education (1962–65); consultant to the National Endowment of the Humanities (1976–); member, United States Commission to UNESCO (1963–69); member of the Executive Committee of the Fédération Internationale des Langues et Littératures Modernes (1967–71), and its American Vice-President (1972–78); chairman of the Conference of Secretaries of the American Council of Learned Societies (1965–68); Distinguished Lecturer for the National Council of Teachers of English (1971–72); member of the Executive Committee of the Modern Humanities Research Association of Great Britain (1972–75); trustee of the Woodrow Wilson National Fellowship Foundation (1972–75); member of the Board of Directors of the American Council of Education (1974); member of the Advisory Committee on the Yale Humanities Institute (1974–75); and University of Tennessee Chancellor's Research Scholar (1979) and Mace Bearer (1987–88).

Throughout this entire period, as he has continued to teach and serve higher education, John has remained an active scholar. He has published many important books and articles on the emergence of standard English, and on Chaucer, Gower, and other literary figures. Derek Brewer called his edition of Chaucer (1977), a "massive achievement." The late distinguished medievalist Francis Lee Utley referred to John's book on John Gower (1964) as "a massive contribution to the study of the fourteenth century." A sign of the value of this rich scholarship is its continual citation. We all await his edition of Chaucer's *Wife of Bath*, for the Chaucer Variorum.

These and other accomplishments have indeed been recognized by the scholarly community. John has been awarded an L.H.D. by Loyola University of Chicago (1970) and a Litt.D from Middlebury College, Vermont (1970). John was elected to Phi Beta Kappa and has served as Senator at Large (1976–) to that organization. He has received many major research fellowships, including those from the National Endowment for the Humanities, and the American Council of Learned Societies.

As I look back over John's illustrious career, I believe the thing that strikes me the most is what all the service and awards point toward: a professional life devoted to serving and furthering the quality of higher education. There is a paradox in this very public professional life of which those who know John are aware—John is a private man not given to self-congratulation. His service to the humanities and to his profession has been his way of replenishing the well of learning. He has remained a gentlemen in an age when that word has become an epithet of a bygone era. He is a loyal friend, a valued colleague, a beloved teacher, and the least selfish man I know.

Standardizing English

Elements of a Written Standard in the Old English Laws

Mary P. Richards

John Fisher's work on the role of Chancery clerks in the emergence of standard written English treats an important aspect of a larger question that has occupied Anglo-Saxon scholars for decades: in a largely oral culture, what function does writing play in the standardization of the language?[1] In his important *Speculum* article, Fisher was concerned primarily with matters of dialect, viz., phonological, morphological, and syntactical features that distinguished Chancery English from regional dialects and foreshadowed the development of Modern English prose. He identified the production of administrative and judicial documents as the source of standardizing tendencies in the English language, beginning in the late thirteenth century.

For Anglo-Saxonists, the search for Standard Old English continues apace. There is no identifiable body such as Chancery to study, nor is there necessarily agreement about what constituted Standard Old English. Those who have studied Old English literature, particularly the prose, develop a sense of a standard literary language, but how to pinpoint its origin, development, and features remains an open issue.[2] In the late nineteenth and early twentieth centuries, a popular and highly influential argument was made for the genesis of Standard Old English in the reign of Ælfred.[3] But in 1933, C. L. Wrenn compared the language in three early West-Saxon manuscripts associated with Ælfred and concluded that the three manuscripts in question were not standardized phonologically and that even the individual manuscripts themselves did not show phonological regularity.[4] More recently, scholars have turned to the evidence of vocabulary preferences and sought to identify standardizing tendencies in literary texts and translations written in close connection with Æthelwold's school at Winchester in the latter part of the tenth century.[5] Their theory is that a literary koiné was consciously developed at Winchester as an outgrowth of the Benedictine Revival, and that this can be defined in terms of word choice, if not dialectal features.

But the types of materials examined by Fisher—those produced for functional purposes by a staff assisting the king—have not been examined for whatever light they can shed on the question of standardization. In the Anglo-Saxon period, these materials are the royal diplomas (in Latin) and legal codes, charters, wills, writs, and related documents (in Old English and Latin). Despite a beneficiary's dependence on written documentation of matters such as grants and the settlement of disputes, the office of Chancery did not exist before the Conquest.[6] In fact, the word *cancellarius* (meaning "royal chancellor") is first attested in England in 1062, and the function of that office before the Conquest remains uncertain.[7] Debate over the existence of some sort of a royal Anglo-Saxon secretariat usually centers on the royal diplomas, records of grants normally made by the king in a public setting before witnesses.[8] There is no question that such Latin documents were issued from the royal household with the knowledge and permission of the king who made the grants.[9] The problem is to learn whether the king employed a chancery/secretariat year-round to produce these materials, or instead called upon select bishops and other trustworthy ecclesiastics after the *witan* (council) had met and the writing of documents needed to be done.[10] The weight of opinion now holds with the view that a permanent staff of clerks worked for the king to maintain the administrative records of government and to retain royal control over the valuable power to issue diplomas.

The question of an Anglo-Saxon chancery becomes less critical, in any event, with reference to Old English materials and to Latin charters with lengthy Old English boundary statements. It is unlikely that all of these were the products of royal assistants, and in fact they usually were written and preserved by the ecclesiastical beneficiary, in the case of grants, or by an ecclesiastical foundation with an interest in legal texts, in the case of the laws.[11] Further, surviving copies of the Old English materials often post-date their origin by at least a century. For charters, wills, and related items this situation poses special problems for language study, because these frequently exist in unique copies which may have been changed or updated in the course of time.[12] In many Anglo-Saxon cartularies, for example, the authority of numerous items is open to question, and the originals have often been lost or destroyed.

The Old English laws, however, provide a body of related materials issued by royal authority over five centuries, surviving in multiple copies, that should give evidence of standardizing tendencies in the language if such existed. In an important recent dissertation directed by Professor Fisher, B. Jane Stanfield demonstrated the potential usefulness of the laws for this type of study by comparing the four extant usable copies of the code of Ælfred and Ine.[13] Whereas Stanfield found a number of shared paleographic features in the treatment of *capitula* (chapter titles) and of the body of the laws, she also found significant linguistic divergences corresponding to the relative chronological distance of a given text from the earliest copy preserved in the Parker manuscript, MS. Corpus Christi College, Cambridge 173. When she pursued the question of standardization and divergence within the texts of the laws, she found the phonological and morphological changes from copy to copy that one would expect over time, yet a remarkable consistency in vocabulary from the earliest copy to the latest version of *Ælfred-Ine*.

Stanfield's conclusions tell us that the Old English laws underwent little significant alteration in vocabulary as they were copied at different times and places. Thus we can be relatively certain that our copies of the codes reflect their original contents, and we can use them to trace the process of borrowing and adaptation implied by Ælfred's preface, which indicates that he looked to codes issued by his royal predecessors when developing his own compendium.[14] From all the evidence, it appears that royal legislation written after Ælfred continued to follow the precedents of previous legislation in vocabulary and, to a great degree, structure and style. An acknowledged sense of tradition, of folk law renewed and brought up to date, gave shape to many of the codes associated with later kings.[15]

This is not to say, however, that the surviving Old English legal codes and collections always represent finished works intended for consultation, as is the case with legislation today. As Wormald has shown, much of what remains from Æthelred's time, for instance, is work in progress, documents in which royal decrees may have been first recorded before being developed by the king's legal draftsman, Archbishop Wulfstan, into statements for his own (ecclesiastical) purposes.[16] Wormald stresses rightly that the word of the law, rather than the letter, was of primary importance in court. In fact, authoritative, comprehensive codes were issued by only two kings: Ælfred and Cnut. Separated by roughly a century and a half, these kings had a keen sense of the tradition of royal legislation in England and on the continent, and their laws reflect the height of that tradition. Although Archbishop Wulfstan did draft most, if not all, of Cnut's legislation, Wulfstan represented the state of the art in the early eleventh century. He assisted the king in asserting his royal authority, even as he drew on earlier legal statements that he himself had written.[17]

Yet, as Stanfield demonstrated, the question of standardization in the Old English laws is intimately bound to their written form. One code looks very like another, despite differences in date of composition and of copy. Thus, before moving to a consideration of specific elements of standardization in the language of the laws, we must review the manuscript contexts in which they are preserved.[18] Surviving materials were produced at ecclesiastical centers, which had an interest in the laws generally. The church, for example, had a major role in the judicial process as the administrator of the ordeal, and the bishop presided jointly with the ealdorman at the shire court.[19] Although copies of royal proclamations may at times have circulated throughout the country so that they could be communicated to the people, especially to those who had responsibility in the various courts, legal materials were collected and occasionally rewritten by churchmen.[20] The church, of course, was the main repository of literacy, and its self-interest was at stake, because ecclesiastical and secular law were intermingled during the Anglo-Saxon period and did not become separate until the time of William I. Indeed, the tie to Mosaic law and, hence, Christian tradition, so effectively drawn by Ælfred in the preface to his code, seems to have operated as a major force to link the church with the laws from the time of the earliest Christian kings of Kent. The point to be made here is that, despite the church's self-interested role in preserving the Old English laws and despite the changing nature of these manuscript compilations over time, the texts of individual codes remain remarkably consistent, so much so that the twelfth-century *Textus Roffensis* produced at Rochester Cathedral Priory often contains the most complete version of a given set of laws. Hence it is possible to compare different copies of a single code, and the texts of various codes, in the process of determining standardizing elements in the written laws.

Beyond its role in preserving the laws, what impact did the church have on the language, structure, and style of the legal codes? Surviving legal collections indicate that the influence was powerful indeed. It was at times editorial: anonymous short codes of later date were frequently added to *Ælfred-Ine*, implying that this code was regarded as a general compendium by copyists.[21] At other times it was more substantive, as the work attributed to Wulfstan indicates.[22] Most importantly, new legislation seems to have been written with earlier materials in mind. That is, whoever put a given set of royal proclamations in written form followed the language and structure of previous codes, which must have been available for reference. Ælfred indicates that he went through just such a process in compiling his own code, and appends a version of Ine's earlier laws as a demonstration of his method. In this case, Ælfred seemingly asked his ecclesiastical councillors to collect whatever examples of earlier codes they could find and to present them to him for consideration. He states expressly that he did not write down his own laws, for he could not be certain which of these might withstand the test of time.[23] More than a century later, Cnut was to give similar instructions to Archbishop Wulfstan. Thus the church, with its resources of materials and clerks, seems to have been an important agent for composing and recording legislation in final form, then maintaining copies of the laws for future consultation.

Which legal codes a given ecclesiastical authority followed when he put new royal legislation into written form does not matter as much as the fact that he followed a tradition at all. Yet, from the times of the earliest kings of Kent, certain traditions influenced the shape and style of the written laws throughout the Anglo-Saxon period. It seems clear that later writers chose to follow these models because they gave authority to new legislation. Thus, although collections like those preserved today existed apart from oral folk law and probably had little influence on the judicial process, they tell us a great deal about a lengthy written legal tradition in Anglo-Saxon England.[24]

What were the formal components of that tradition? First and most obvious is the structure of the royal codes, which resembles that of certain continental Germanic codes, most notably the *Lex Salica* and the *Lex Burgundia*.[25] Like their Frankish predecessors, Old English legal statements of more than a few sentences open normally with a preface that provides a context for the list that follows. The preface usually conveys an indication of the proximity of the written law's creation to the time of its pronouncement. In some cases, the opening statements are summary: "These are the decrees which King Æthelberht established in the lifetime of Augustine."[26] In others, a specific occasion is mentioned: it may be a scourge such as the plague (*IV Eadgar*) or the Vikings (*II Æthelred, VII Æthelred*), a peace settlement (*Ælfred and Guthrum, Eadward and Guthrum*), or, more frequently, a meeting of the king and his councillors. When a meeting is mentioned, an ecclesiastical official usually is named, and the details given about the meeting provide clues to its proximity to the text. For example, the opening statement to Wihtred's Kentish code conveys considerably more information about the circumstances under which the decrees originated than do the prologues to the earlier Kentish codes. There is no reason to think that this information was a later addition, despite the fact that all three Kentish codes survive only in a unique, twelfth-century copy. The man who wrote down

Wihtred's legislation seems to have had first-hand information about the council:

> During the sovereignty of Wihtred, the most gracious king of Kent, in the fifth year of his reign, the ninth Indiction, the sixth day of Rugern, in a place which is called Barham, there was assembled a deliberative council of the notables. There were present there Berhtwald, the chief bishop of Britain, and the above-mentioned king; the bishop of Rochester, who was called Gefmund; and every order of the Church of the province expressed itself in unanimity with the loyal laity [assembled there]. . . .[27]

Not every preface is so specific about the occasion of the code. Ælfred's and Cnut's laws, for example, are compendia of earlier codes which are selected, arranged, and amplified with the guidance of their councillors. These are not meant to be proclamations, but summaries of the laws operative under their rule, as their prefaces indicate. Certain other royal codes, however, embody moral and religious exhortations. The preface to *II Eadmund* contains a statement, attributed to the king, that he has been considering the best means to promote Christianity. Thereafter follows a list of punishments for homicide, vendetta, and violation of a household, in the midst of which is a statement of thanks for the suppression of thievery in the kingdom. *X Æthelred*, written by Archbishop Wulfstan, is a more general exhortation to the people to uphold their faith and promote justice, and it opens with a preface very similar to that of *II Eadmund*. Thus, while preambles to codes vary according to the occasion and subject matter, they follow the pattern of earlier codes of the same type. Even when a preamble adopts the first person, its language is formulaic:

> *II Eadmund*: ðæt ic smeade mid minra witena geðeahte, . . . hu ic
> mæhte Cristendomes maest aræran. (186)
> *X Æthelred*: ic Æðelred cyning ærest smeade, hu ic Cristendom
> æfre mihte 7 rihtne cynedom fyrmest aræran. . . . (269)

As this comparison demonstrates, even Wulfstan, whose distinctive style betrays his authorship, began writing codes associated with two kings (Æthelred and Cnut) using Old English legal formulae.[28]

As in Germanic law, the Old English codes typically follow the preface with a series of individual statements. These may be numbered in a given MS., as those of Ælfred and Ine usually are, or they may be rubricated with titles. When titles occur, they often refer to the subject of the following statement or to the ruler with whom it is associated. *Ælfred-Ine* receives the most elaborate treatment of any of the codes. It has a list of contents along with an extended preface, and the codes of both kings are treated as a single series. Because the combined codes cover a wide range of crimes and punishments, the list of contents is needed for reference. Indeed, the MS. presentation suggests that *Ælfred-Ine* was understood and used as a formal unit. This situation may have influenced Liebermann's belief that the phrase "seo domboc" in later codes always referred to *Ælfred-Ine*.[29] Liebermann's interpretation is now disputed by Dafydd Jenkins, who finds that, in certain instances, the items said to be treated in "seo domboc" do not appear in *Ælfred-Ine*.[30] Jenkins instead proposes that *domboc* meant any book of judgments, not one necessarily connected to a king.

When we examine the extant references to "seo domboc," however, some interesting patterns emerge to indicate that both Liebermann and Jenkins are correct:

> *I Eadward* pref.: Eadwerd cyning byt ðam gerefum eallum, ðæt ge deman swa rihte domas swa ge rihtoste cunnon, 7 hit on ðære dombec stande. Ne wandiað for nanum ðingum folcriht to geregceanne. . . . (138)
>
> *II Eadward* 5: Gif hwa ðis oferhebbe 7 his að 7 his wæd brece, ðe eal ðeod geseald haefð, bete swa domboc tæce. (142)
>
> *II Æthelstan* 5: 7 we cwædon be ciricbryce: gif he ful wære on ðam ðryfealdan ordale, bete be þam þe sio domboc secge. (152)
>
> *II Eadgar* 5: 7 healde man ælces Sunnandæges freols fram nontide þaes Sæternesdæges oð ðæs Monandæges lihtinge, be þam wite, þe domboc tæcð. . . . (198)

The first of these examples comes close to stating that "seo domboc" was consulted in written form by those charged with administering justice, though the list of judgments could have been known in a variety of ways. It further distinguishes the written reference (*domboc*) from popular law (*folcriht*), and implies that the latter depends on the former for enactment. In the three subsequent examples, however, "domboc" is the subject of an active verb, much as words referring to the Gospels or the Bible are used in other contexts in Old English. The earliest mention of "seo domboc" in the preface to Eadward's first code does seem to imply *Ælfred-Ine*, which is a compendium of punishments covering a wide set of circumstances arising in society. Because of its proximity in date to Eadward's reign, *Ælfred-Ine* likely would have been known to the author of *I Eadward*, and it seems designed to serve the function implied in the preface, that is, to provide an operative written tradition in support of oral law. By the time *II Eadward* was written, *domboc* had entered the formulaic language of the laws and may already have become generalized to mean a compendium of judgments.

With reference to manuscript presentation, the major variable in treatments of *Ælfred-Ine* is the addition of certain short anonymous codes to the basic collection, such as the statement of ordeals for incendiaries and murderers.[31] By comparison, a less comprehensive code, *II Æthelstan* (925 X 935), shows variation in title that can be tied to the purposes and aims of the manuscript contexts in which the code appears. In the historically organized *Textus Roffensis* the title is "Æthelstanes gerænesse [*sic*]," whereas in the topically arranged MS. Corpus Christi College, Cambridge 383, the code opens with the rubric "Be ðeofum," the subject of its first five statements. These codices are roughly contemporary, from the first half of the twelfth century, and seem to have been produced within the same general region, Rochester and London.[32] Rubrics to subsequent groups of statements in *II Æthelstan* do not always appear, but in most cases space has been left for a rubric at the corresponding place in the manuscript where the phrase itself is missing. This suggests that, although the titles of the code differ in the two manuscripts, the copyists were following a text with a common format. In yet another variation of the pattern, the codes of Æthelred and Cnut, which survive in multiple copies, are never numbered and rarely rubricated, but most of the individual statements begin with "and," a device that emphasizes their function as a type of list.

These three examples demonstrate that an individual code could have its own scheme of division and that this scheme ordinarily remained constant through successive recopyings. Robinson has noted similarities between the Old English laws and other types of records kept in lists, such as chronicles and genealogies.[33] The difference between these historical records and the laws is that the order of the statements remains constant only within a given legal code; the various royal codes do not follow a standard historical arrangement in the manuscript collections.

There are similarities in the style of the laws, too, suggesting that their authors looked to earlier codes for models when they put the king's pronouncements into written form for preservation. Beginning with the earliest laws from Kent and continuing through Æthelred, the most prominent stylistic feature of the laws is the "Gif" clause stating the crime, followed by the appropriate punishment:

> *Æthelberht* 20: Gif man þone man ofslæhð, XX scillingum
>   gebete. (4)
> *Ælfred* 48: Gif mon oðrum þæt neb ofaslea, gebete him mid LX
>   scill'. (80)
> *II Æthelstan* 20.7: Gif hwa hine wrecan wille oððe hine fælæce,
>   þonne beo he fah wið ðone cyng 7 wið ealle his freond. (160)
> *III Eadgar* 7.2: 7 gyf aðor oððe mæg oþþe fremde þa rade forsace,
>   gylde þam cynge hundtwelftig scill'. (204)
> *VI Æthelred* 39: 7 gif hwa nunnan gewemme oþþe wydewan
>   nydnæme, gebete þæt deope for Gode 7 for worolde. (256)

In the royal codes, the "Gif" clauses come to be used less frequently over time as the codes evolve in nature from lists of crimes and punishments to hortative and moralistic statements authored by Wulfstan, but these clauses continue to appear as late as Cnut's reign, even as more complex legal statements develop.

Another traditional stylistic feature of the laws is the use of the first person in legal statements. Ine's codes are the earliest in which this feature is found, and its pattern is typical of later royal codes. The first-person singular pronoun *ic* occurs in the prologue, but subsequent statements use *we*, the plural form. Thus, although the introduction to a code may be couched as a personal message from the king, the actual code usually signals the collected wisdom of the king and his councillors. An important exception, however, is the use of "ic wille" in codes such as *II Eadward* and *I Æthelstan*. In these examples, the first-person singular construction introduces a statement concerning men who serve the king in government: reeves, property-holders, and bishops.[34] Further, despite the fact that the laws as preserved are often literary renditions of royal proclamations, they contain hints of their oral origins in these first-person constructions. The phrase "we beodaþ" occurs repeatedly as early as Ine's laws and as late as the laws of Cnut, as does "we læraþ" from Ælfred through Cnut. The most widespread phrase of all is "we cwædon," which appears so frequently in certain royal codes such as *I Eadward* as to seem formulaic. Such phrases serve as reminders of the orality of the laws and indicate that even those who committed the codes to writing understood them as having authority through the spoken word as much as in their written form.[35] Once again the force of tradition becomes clear in the work of Wulfstan, for whom the written word held great significance as he revised royal legislation and composed other legal codes not associated with kings; at the same time, he employed the phraseology of earlier codes that implied oral pronouncements rather than a finished written product:

> *VI Æthelred* 5: 7 ealle Godes þeowas, 7 huruþinga sacerdas, we
>   biddað 7 læraþ, þæt hy Gode hyran 7 clænnesse lufian 7
>   beorhgan him sylfum wið Godes yrre. (248)
> *I Cnut* 7: And we lærað 7 biddað 7 on Godes naman
>   beodað. . . . (290)

In her important article written more than fifty years ago, Bethurum surveyed stylistic features of the Old English laws and provided examples of alliterative formulae found in these texts, from which she posited oral origins for the laws.[36] It is worth noting, however, that the preponderance of cited formulae occur in codes associated with Wulfstan, especially *V*, *VI*, and *VII Æthelred* and *I–II Cnut*. We can speculate that the formulaic tendencies of the earlier laws were consonant with Wulfstan's affinity for alliterating word-pairs so prominent in his homiletic writing. Hence the most formulaic Old English legislation actually is among the latest in date and can be tied to an author who wrote many works for oral delivery. As a stylist, Wulfstan may actually have been closer to the oral language of the laws than those writing legislation before him.[37]

Thus far our focus has been on the structure and style of the Old English royal codes, which seem to have been written down over the centuries following a very old, probably imported, tradition. Although similarities among the codes have been stressed, we have not overlooked changes that developed through time. Two features of these changes are worthy of note: first, they occur within the general traditional framework of the written laws, such that the new codes remain clearly identifiable as part of the longer tradition; second, variations in style appear gradually, with the result that older forms are not supplanted but decrease in frequency of occurrence. These features bespeak a written tradition of the law, probably one that took place within an ecclesiastical setting. The production of related historical materials, such as the Anglo-Saxon Chronicle, genealogies, and regnal and episcopal lists, certainly did so, and the Church is associated closely with most such materials having traditional form during the Anglo-Saxon period.

The question remains, was the vocabulary of the laws subject to the same types of standardizing influences that we have identified in the structure and style of the codes? Many of the examples quoted thus far in the present study would indicate so, but the matter of vocabulary is a complex one. In previous studies of Æthelwold's vocabulary developed at Winchester in the tenth century, words examined for standardizing tendencies often had Latin equivalents. Where certain Old English word choices had been made in the course of translating from the Latin, initial judgments about vocabulary preferences could be reached. The Old English laws, however, are in their original language; most

Latin versions did not appear until the Norman period. Furthermore, their subjects are secular as well as ecclesiastical; hence they include a fairly broad range of vocabulary. The laws embody a large technical vocabulary, too, as they attempt to specify crimes, punishments, and the manner in which guilt or innocence is proven. In trying to survey the vocabulary of the laws for comparative purposes, then, it seems that we must examine three broad categories of word choices: those having Latin equivalents, those having widespread general usage in the language, and those having technical meaning limited primarily to the laws.

To begin with Latin equivalents, Gneuss has cited the use of *weofod* for Latin *altar* as characteristic of the "Winchester group" of preferences. Although this is true for Winchester, Hofstetter has noted that *weofod* also occurs outside the temporal and geographic boundaries of Æthelwold's school.[38] The Old English term seems to be of pagan origin (< *wig* + *beod* = "sacrifice place"), and is found in two of the Kentish codes (*Hlothhere and Eadric* 16, 2; *Wihtred* 8 and 18–21). Ælfred uses *weofod* in his preface (13), and it becomes the standard term in later royal codes, including the preface to the English version of the Coronation Oath, where, however, *weofod* has no equivalent in the Latin version; *VII Æthelred* 6, 3; and in compounds such as *weofodbot* (*II Cnut* 42) and *weofodþegn* (*VIII Æthelred* 18; 22; 28; *II Cnut* 39; 41). In the anonymous laws, such as the Old English rituals for the ordeal, *weofod* again is the preferred term. Indeed, it appears throughout the royal codes as the only word for *altar*. Whatever the range of its usage, this word clearly was regarded as part of the standard legal vocabulary to be used by writers as late as Wulfstan in composing legal statements.

Words indicating "guilt," "sin," and "offense" in the laws form a striking pattern that again suggests a traditional vocabulary for legal statements. With the exception of *misdæda*, which appears several times in the codes of Æthelred and Cnut, *synne* is the ecclesiastical term in the laws. Otherwise, *scyld* and *scyldig*, meaning "offense" and "guilty," predominate from the time of the Kentish laws through the codes of Cnut. *Gylt*, the Winchester preference over *scyld*, occurs in four instances: in the laws of Ine (73), Ælfred (5.4 and 7.1), and Æthelstan (II, 8), where it means "offense."

Certain other ecclesiastical terms, however, reveal different patterns in the laws. One finds *husl* and *huslgang* referring to the sacraments, but these have no other equivalents in Old English. With the exception of one instance in Ælfred's code (8), *mynster* ("monastery") and *cirice* ("church") are kept separate in meaning until the time of Wulfstan, who seems to generalize the former, as in *V Æthelred* 12, 1. His statement, echoed again in *VI Æthelred* 21 and *I Cnut* 13, 1, directs payment for the soul of the dead to be made to the church (*mynster*) to which an individual belonged, even if that person died in another parish. *I Æthelstan* 4, the earliest statement on *sawlsceat*, uses *cirice*. Again, *preost* is the usual word for "priest" until the later legislation written by Archbishop Wulfstan (*VI Æthelred*, *I Cnut*), in which *sacerd* appears occasionally. These examples indicate that standardizing tendencies in vocabulary choices did not operate exclusively, and the choices reflected in the laws did not always indicate a preferred legal vocabulary. But within the laws, a strong tradition can also be seen even on the level of general vocabulary, as will be clear from the evidence to follow.

In the royal codes, the preferred word meaning "to give, deliver, or relinquish" is *agiefan*, as opposed to *giefan* or *gesellan*. *Agiefan* occurs frequently in the earlier codes and continues to appear through Cnut. When, however, compensation is associated with the verb of giving, *gesellan* is the preferred term:

> *Ælfred* 64, 4: Gif sio lytle ta sie ofaslegen, geselle him V scill. (84)
> *II Cnut* 63: Gyf hwa reaflac gewyrce, agyfe 7 forgylde, 7 beo his weres scyldig wið þone cingc. (352)

Forms of *sellan* also appear, most often meaning "sell," but in a few instances, the usage overlaps that of *agiefan*: *Wihtred* 22, and *Ælfred* 5, 2 and 42, 4.

Also interesting is the word *nied/neod*, which is used to imply compulsion in the earlier laws, and continues with this meaning as late as the codes of Cnut (*II Cnut* 68, 2). In the codes authored by Wulfstan, however, *nied* comes to be used equally as often in its more general sense "need," though the verb *niedan* continues to mean "compel," and *nied* in compound forms implies involuntary action.[39] Likewise, *folc* occurs infrequently before Wulfstan and appears most often in compounds such as *folcland*, *folcriht*, and *folcgemot*. This is a popular word with homilists, as opposed to those who composed laws, and hence it creeps into the Archbishop's legal prose in the phrase "Christen folc."

Liebermann remains the best explicator of Old English legal terminology.[40] For a number of legal terms alternative words were available in the Old English lexicon, yet one preferred form became traditional in the laws. The predominant terms for "accuse" and "accusation" in the royal codes are *tihtan/tihtlian*, *tihte*, and the adjective *tihtbysig*, meaning "often accused," hence "having a bad reputation." Some form of the word occurs in virtually every code and serves as part of the technical vocabulary of the laws. An alternate to *tihtan* and *tihtlian* is *teon* < *tihan*, also meaning "accuse." The latter occurs infrequently and might have been confused with the dominant forms. For example, one finds

> *III Æthelred* 8: And ælc mynetere, þe man tihð, þæt fals feoh
> sloge. . . . (230)
> *III Æthelred* 13: 7 gif man hwilcne man teo, þæt he þone man fede,
> þe ures hlafordes grið tobrocen habbe. . . . (230)

where *tihð* and *teo* seem to have the same meaning, though the latter is subjunctive in mood. Elsewhere in the code, forms such as *betihlod*, *tihtbysig*, and *tiond* ("accuser") appear. Alternatives to the dominant form, such as *onsprecan*, occur sporadically, and indicate that, although variants were known to the authors of the laws, they preferred the form traditional since Kentish times.

Mæg (pl. *magas*) is the word most often used to mean "kinsman." The codes of Æthelstan and *II Eadmund* alternate *mægð*, a collective form of *mæg*, with the plural, but other terms such as *cynne* do not appear until the codes of Æthelred, and then only infrequently. On the other hand, *lagu* ("law"), probably a Scandinavian borrowing, first appears in the codes of Edgar, and in its early uses refers not to royal legislation but to the Danelaw.[41]

The preferred terms for royal codes were *dom* and *æw* until Wulf-stan began using *lagu* more broadly and dropped *æw* except in compounds. We can speculate that, after the enactment of the Danelaw < *Denalagu*, the form *lagu* gained wider currency and lost its more restrictive meanings. As evidence of this, twelfth-century manuscripts often use this newer term in rubrics (*Ælfredes laga cyninges*). It is also possible that the authors of legislation after Ælfred, especially Wulfstan, thought that they were follow-ing traditional usage, since the Danelaw was so closely linked with Ælfred and his accomplishments as a ruler.

Another instance where a significant legal term changed, this time early in its history, can be found in the words for "ordeal." *Ordal*, referring to the religious ceremony used to determine the guilt or innocence of the accused, occurs first in *II Æthelstan* and thereafter becomes the standard term for the ritual. Prior to this, Ine's code had used the word *ceace* seemingly to refer to some type of test or trial, though perhaps not in a religious context. The earliest manuscript preserving Ine's code, MS. Corpus Christi College, Cambridge 173, reads *ceape* for *ceace* in every instance, however, and the context seems to imply an exchange of goods to avoid trial by ordeal:

> *Ine* 62: Ðonne mon bið tyhtlan betygen, 7 hine mon bedrifeð to ceape*, nah þonne self nane wiht to gesellane beforan ceape*: þonne gaeþ oðer mon, seleð his ceap fore, swa he þonne geþingian mæge, on ða rædenne, þe he him ga to honda, oð ðæt he his ceap him geinnian mæge: þonne betyhð hine mon eft oþre siðe 7 bedrifð to ceape*: gif hine for nele forstandan se ðe him ær ceap foresealde, 7 he hine þonne forfehð, þolige þonne his ceapes se, ðe he him ær foresealde. (116)
> *Reads *ceace* in MSS. other than CCCC 173.

Liebermann prefers the reading *ceace* found in the twelfth-century MSS., which he translates as "kettle," the vessel to be used in an ordeal of hot water. The problem with Liebermann's interpreta-tion is that *ceace*, meaning "vessel," is never used elsewhere in Old English to refer to an ordeal.[42] When used in a religious con-text, it seems to imply a ritual purification, never a trial. These points are raised here to indicate that the standard term in the laws, *ordal*, is not, strictly speaking, the earliest word for trial by ordeal, but it certainly is the technical term used exclusively in the royal codes to refer to the ceremony conducted under the auspices of the church from the early tenth century onwards. It is Germanic in origin, rather than Latin, and so may have been applied to the distinctive ceremony which continued into the post-Conquest period.

There are many other examples from the technical vocabulary of the laws that could be cited in support of the argument that a traditional vocabulary operated in the royal codes over time, but this evidence is finally the least significant, for we would expect this category of language to be consistent before all others. It is worth reiterating here, however, that numerous legal concepts never were restricted to a single term, and that a cluster of terms, such as *grið*, *friþ*, and *pax*, could be used for the same concept from the time of the earliest codes. In more general terminology, no single word for "child" is preferred; *bearn*, *cild*, and *cniht* are equally popular. The language of the written laws, then, is best described as a series of vocabulary preferences—some having Latin equivalents, some having general meaning, and others technical—that occur from code to code and imply that the authors of those laws understood they were writing traditional material that required a traditional vocabulary.

When the moment came to enter those codes into formal codices, the copyists followed a traditional format that in itself communicated the nature of the material presented, just as can be seen in the versions of the Anglo-Saxon Chronicle. Further, the authors of royal legislation seem to have been well versed in the style and structure, as well as the vocabulary, of earlier codes. One can easily perceive how the Anglo-Saxon Chronicle, with entries added from year to year, could engender a sustained format. In order to understand the style, structure, and even manuscript presentation of the Old English laws, however, one must posit familiarity with a variety of earlier texts, gained at the cost of some effort by the author and perhaps the copyist as well. On the basis of the surviving evidence, it is reasonable to speculate that only a few ecclesiastical centers, those closely associated with one or more kings, played a role in producing legal collections of the type that would support continued work on these materials. Manuscripts associated with Archbishop Wulfstan are helpful here, because they show the variety of materials he drew upon to support his legal writing at Worcester or York.[43] If we understand the Old English laws to have been composed and preserved formally at relatively few centers, we can begin to see why, as a body of materials, they seem so closely related to one another despite having been written over the course of five centuries. In other words, the standardizing elements in the laws probably emerge from the environment in which they were written, for the effort to follow traditional models produced a high degree of uniformity in the materials, a uniformity worthy of the later office of Chancery.

NOTES

1. "Chancery and the Emergence of Standard Written English in the Fifteenth Century," *Speculum* 52 (1977):870–99. Fisher expands the scope of this work in "European Chancelleries and the Rise of Standard Written Languages," *Proceedings of The Illinois Medieval Association* 3 (1986):1–33. The present study relies on *A Microfiche Concordance to Old English*, ed. Richard L. Venezky and Antonette diPaolo Healey (Newark: University of Delaware, 1980) for its discussion of the frequency and context of vocabulary items in the Old English laws. The standard edition of the laws is by Felix Liebermann, *Die Gesetze der Angelsachsen*, 3 vols. (Halle: Niemeyer, 1903–16; rpt. 1960). All quotations in Old English are drawn from Liebermann's first version of the text in question, as edited in volume 1.

2. These issues are explored at length in Helmut Gneuss, "The origin of Standard Old English and Æthelwold's school at Winchester," *Anglo-Saxon England* 1 (1972):63–83.

3. *King Alfred's West-Saxon Version of Gregory's 'Pastoral Care'*, ed. Henry Sweet, Early English Text Society O. S. 45, 50 (London, 1871), 1:v–vi.

4. " 'Standard' Old English," *Transactions of the Philological Society*, 1933, 65–88.

5. See Gneuss, especially pp. 75–78; the notes to his article indicate the scope of problems under consideration by his students at the University of Munich.

6. On Anglo-Saxon dispute settlement, see Patrick Wormald, "Charters, Law and the Settlement of Disputes in Anglo-Saxon England" in *The Settlement of Disputes in Early Medieval Europe*, ed. Wendy Davies and Paul Fouracre (Cambridge: Cambridge University Press, 1986), 149–68. Simon Keynes argues for the existence of a royal secretariat during the reign of King Æthelred in *The Diplomas of King Æthelred 'The Unready' 978–1016* (Cambridge: Cambridge University Press, 1980).

7. *Dictionary of Medieval Latin from British Sources*, Fasc. 2:C, ed. R. E. Latham (London: The British Academy, 1981), 255.

8. The earliest to raise the question of an Anglo-Saxon chancery were W. H. Stevenson, "An Old English Charter," *English Historical Review* 11 (1896):731–44; Hubert Hall, *Studies in English Official Historical Documents* (1908; rpt. New York: Burt Franklin, 1969), 175, 189; and Richard Drögereit, "Gab es eine angelsächsische Königskanzlei?" *Arkiv für Urkundenforschung* 13 (1935):335–426. A good summary of recent research is found in Nicholas Brooks, "Anglo-Saxon Charters: The Work of the Last Twenty Years," *Anglo-Saxon England* 3 (1974): 217–20.

9. *English Historical Documents c. 500–1042*, ed. Dorothy Whitelock, 2nd. ed. (London: Eyre Methuen, 1979), 376–80.

10. For the view that Anglo-Saxon kings used bishops and other ecclesiastics to handle their charters, see three works by Pierre Chaplais: "The Origin and Authenticity of the Royal Anglo-Saxon Diploma," *Journal of the Society of Archivists* 3, no. 4 (1965):48–61; "The Anglo-Saxon Chancery: From the Diploma to the Writ," *Journal of the Society of Archivists* 3, no. 4 (1966):160–76; and "The Royal Anglo-Saxon 'Chancery' of the Tenth Century Revisited," in *Studies in Medieval History Presented to R. H. C. Davis* (London and Ronceverte, WV: The Hambledon Press, 1985), 41–51.

11. See the introduction and descriptions in *Medieval Cartularies of Great Britain*, ed. G. R. C. Davis (London: Longmans, Green, 1958); and David Walker, "The Organization of Material in Medieval Cartularies," in *The Study of Medieval Records* (Essays in honour of Kathleen Major), ed. D. A. Bullough and R. L. Story (Oxford: Clarendon Press, 1971), 132–50. On the laws, see Patrick Wormald, "Æthelred the Lawmaker," in *Ethelred the Unready: Papers from the Millenary Conference*, ed. David Hill, B A R British Series 59 (1978), 47–80.

12. Whitelock discusses the matter of authenticity of extant charters in *EHD* 1:369–75. See also the entries in P. H. Sawyer, *Anglo-Saxon Charters* (London: Royal Historical Society, 1968). An instructive analysis of the extant Anglo-Saxon charters from a single house is given by A. Campbell in *Charters of Rochester* (London: The British Academy, 1973), xxii–xxvii.

13. "Standardization in the Anglo-Saxon Laws: A Diplomatic Study" (Ph.D. diss., University of Tennessee, 1984).

14. This point is documented in detail by Pauline Stafford in "The Laws of Cnut and the History of Anglo-Saxon Royal Promises," *Anglo-Saxon England* 10 (1981):173–90.

15. Dorothy Bethurum, "Stylistic Features of the Old English Laws," *Modern Language Review* 27 (1932):263–79. As Dafydd Jenkins argues in "The Medieval Welsh Idea of Law," *Tijdschrift voor Rechtsgeschiedenis* 49 (1981):323–48, the Anglo-Saxon kings did not intend to create new law, but to revitalize the "good old law."

16. Wormald, "Æthelred the Lawmaker," 51–58.

17. See Stafford, "The laws of Cnut;" Dorothy Whitelock, "Wulfstan and the Laws of Cnut," *English Historical Review* 63 (1948):433–52; "Wulfstan's Authorship of Cnut's Laws," *English Historical Review* 70 (1955):72–85; A. G. Kennedy, "Cnut's law code of 1018," *Anglo-Saxon England* 11 (1983):57–81.

18. For a full discussion of the topic, see Mary P. Richards, "The Manuscript Contexts of the Old English Laws: Tradition and Innovation," in *Studies in Earlier Old English Prose*, ed. Paul E. Szarmach (Albany, N.Y.: SUNY Press, 1986), 171–92.

19. Pauline A. Stafford, "Church and Society in the Age of Ælfric," in *The Old English Homily and Its Backgrounds*, ed. Paul E. Szarmach and Bernard F. Huppé (Albany, N.Y.: SUNY Press, 1978), 21.

20. In her article "Gesetzgebung und Schriftlichkeit—Das Beispiel der angelsächsischen Gesetze," Hanna Vollrath argues that the directions for circulating *IV Edgar* are so specific as to suggest that this practice was infrequent (*Historisches Jahrbuch* 99 [1979]:46–47.) See also on the role of memory in the living law, M. T. Clanchy, "Remembering the Past and the Good Old Law," *History* 55 (1970):165–76.

21. Richards, 174–85.

22. Wormald, "Æthelred the Lawmaker," 70, 76.

23. Liebermann 1:46.

24. Clanchy, 172. These ideas are developed at greater length in his

book *From Memory to Written Record. England 1066–1307* (London: Edward Arnold, 1979).

25. J. M. Wallace-Hadrill, *Early Germanic Kingship in England and on the Continent* (Oxford: Clarendon Press, 1971), 33–9. The influence of *Lex Salica* is stressed by Patrick Wormald in "*Lex Scripta* and *Verbum Regis*: Legislation and Germanic Kingship, from Euric to Cnut," in *Early Medieval Kingship*, ed. P. H. Sawyer and I. N. Wood (Leeds: University of Leeds, 1977), 105–38. See also Rosamond McKitterick, "Some Carolingian Law-Books and their Function," in *Authority and Power*, ed. Brian Tierney and Peter Lineham (Cambridge: Cambridge University Press, 1980), 13–27.

26. *The Laws of the Earliest English Kings*, ed. and trans. F. L. Attenborough (Cambridge: Cambridge University Press, 1922), 5.

27. Ibid., 25.

28. On collections of legal materials associated with Wulfstan, see Richards, 176–81, and Dorothy Bethurum, "Archbishop Wulfstan's Commonplace Book," *PMLA* 57 (1942):916–29.

29. Liebermann, 3:93.

30. Jenkins, 343–45. Ælfred's concern for just judgments is portrayed vividly by his biographer Asser, whose work is now available in translation; see Simon Keynes and Michael Lapidge, *Alfred the Great* (Middlesex: Penguin, 1983), 109–10.

31. Liebermann, 1:388.

32. Richards, 181–86.

33. Fred C. Robinson, "Old English Literature in Its Most Immediate Context," in *Old English Literature in Context: Ten Essays*, ed. John Niles (Bury St. Edmunds: D. S. Brewer, 1980), 26.

34. *II Eadweard* 4, 8; *I Æthelstan* 1, 4, 5.

35. Wormald, "*Lex Scripta*," 123–4, and Clanchy, "Remembering the Past," 172.

36. See n15 above.

37. Dorothy Whitelock, "Wulfstan and the so-called Laws of Edward and Guthrum," *English Historical Review* 56 (1941):17–19.

38. Walter Hofstetter, private communication. See further Hoffstetter's *Winchester und der spätaltenglische Sprachgebrauch. Untersuchungen zur geographischen und zeitlichen Verbreitung altenglischer Synonyme*. Texte und Untersuchen für Englischen Philologie. Band 14. Munich, 1987.

39. E.g. *niedgafol* "tribute"; *niednaman* "rape, assault"; *niedwyrhta*

"an involuntary agent." The exception to the trend noted here occurs in *Ælfred and Guthrum* 5, where *nied* is used in the general sense.

40. See *Die Gesetze*, v. 2.

41. M. R. Godden, "Ælfric's Changing Vocabulary," *English Studies* 61 (1980):214–17.

42. See *Concordance*.

43. See Bethurum, "Archbishop Wulfstan's Commonplace Book;" Mary Bateson, "A Worcester Cathedral Book of Ecclesiastical Collections, Made c. 1000 A.D.," *English Historical Review* 10 (1895):712–31; Richards, 176–81; Whitelock, *English Historical Documents* 1:364.

Sources of Standardisation in Later Middle English

J. D. Burnley

The historical circumstances attending the emergence of written Standard English are by now quite well known, at least in general outline. In the early decades of the fifteenth century, as French was progressively abandoned as the language of official business, it was replaced by a kind of English employed by those clerks who, as studies on the London population have suggested, continued a tradition of immigration from the East Midlands.[1] In particular, the hundred and twenty or so clerks of Chancery, through their apprenticeship system, established a kind of spelling and morphology which became sufficiently generalised in the fifteenth century to be regarded as a standard.[2] "Chancery Standard," which as an orthographical phenomenon should in principle be kept distinct from the exclusively palaeographical concept of Chancery script, surpassed in its influence all other competing standards that had begun to emerge during the late fourteenth century, among them two "incipient standards" in the London area, and also the Wycliffite Standard in the North Midlands.[3]

With regard to the standardisation of later Middle English, however, this brief outline leaves many important questions unasked. Why did the Chancery Standard succeed rather than any of the others? What in any case is implied by the phrase "Standard English" in this context? In modern times, the phrase denotes a form of language—that is of its phonology, morphology, syntax, and lexis—which is superordinate to geographically variant forms, and which is realised in both spoken and written modes, and in the latter by a consistent orthography. Middle English standards, however, differ sharply from this modern conception, firstly in that they exist, and existed, *only* in the written mode, for standardisation in spoken English belongs to a much later period; and for this reason the use of the word "standard" to refer to Middle English usually implies reference solely to the orthography. Secondly, they are distinct in that the consistency of their orthography does not approach that of Modern Standard English. This latter is especially true of the two languages which Samuels called "incipient standards" of Types II and III, and which are preserved in London manuscripts of the end of the fourteenth century. Rather than exhibiting a perfectly consistent orthography, they have for many words a limited repertoire of permissable spelling variants. It is indeed debatable whether these Types can be called standards at all, for there is no suggestion that they had any official status or central regulation. Nor did they compete as alternative standards within fourteenth-century London, since, although there is some overlap in their chronology, Type III follows very rapidly upon Type II so that the succession appears to represent an evolutionary process in the population of clerks active in London, a process by which East Midland influences superseded earlier influences from East Anglia in modifying an originally Essex-London substratum.

Wycliffite writings and the products of Chancery, by contrast, achieved the basic requirements necessary to be regarded as true standards: a high degree of internal consistency in spelling and a wide dissemination outside the centres which produced them. The fact that both Chancery and Wycliffite writings stem from discernible centres has two effects which are of special importance in establishing a standard: firstly the centres provided the regulation necessary for consistency in orthography, which is the essential precursor of standardisation, and secondly they furnished an identifiable provenance for the distinctive style which, in a medieval context, consistency created.[4] The association of the style with its particular origin may then provide the motivation for its adoption or rejection by new users. Seen in this light, the religious intolerance towards Lollardry which became virulent after 1401, and which it may be assumed was an institutionalisation of more widely felt attitudes, would have militated against the adoption of the Wycliffite standard by any except the ideologically committed. Chancery Standard was hampered by no such deterrent associations, and indeed, as we shall see, had other advantages in the struggle for acceptance.

The ultimate success of a written standard orthography depends firstly on the development of a relatively consistent spelling system permitting few enough variants for its characteristic spellings to be readily recognised as systematic and capable of being imitated, and secondly upon some motivating factor which will persuade prospective users to adopt it. Standardisation, then, has both a linguistic descriptive dimension to do with the technique of representation in writing, and a sociolinguistic one concerned with the breadth of its use. In the case of Chancery Standard, considerable attention has been paid to the former aspect, but much less to the latter.[5] In this paper, therefore, I should like to raise the question whether we can perceive among early fifteenth-century users of English, and especially among literate clerks, any evidence of a climate of opinion propitious for the acceptance and extension of a standard in the broader sense, an intellectual and cultural disposition to match the mechanical extension of the orthography of Chancery. The investigation will pose three questions: Firstly, what indications are there of a concern among literate people for consistency in the spelling of English? Secondly, is there any contemporary recognition of the desirability of a standardised form of written English? And, thirdly, what are the motivations underlying the adoption of standardised forms more generally? The first of these questions I shall approach by examining one aspect of scribal practice in those manuscripts of Chaucer's work which were written in the first decades of the fifteenth century.

Ordinarily, manuscripts produced within a scriptorium may be expected to have been subject to the "house style" of the institution. This may operate at the level of graphology, as Vance Ramsey has recently demonstrated with regard to the writing of the Chaucerian scribes, Geoffrey Spirleng and his son, both scriveners of Norwich, whose hands are so similar that palaeographers find them extremely difficult to distinguish.[6] It may be extended also to the orthographical representation of the sounds and morphology of the language, as already in local standards such as the AB language of the *Ancrene Wisse* and associated texts. Productions of organised scriptoria were often subject to the attentions of a corrector, who made good any omissions and occasionally altered spellings or even replaced words by more intelligible forms. The rubricator, too, seeing an obvious error in spelling, sometimes felt it his duty to make his own corrections. Thus, in the mechanism of text production within the scriptorium, there existed throughout the Middle Ages some regard for consistency and communicative efficiency, and, consequently, a notion of correctness in orthography within limited localities. However, when a work was copied outside the area of its origin, new habits of spelling were imposed, so that works may be in effect translated from one dialect to another, sometimes with great diligence, but more often resulting in a mixed language lacking all consistency.[7] The resulting variety of language within texts is matched by the variety in the practice of individual scribes, among whom consistency in spelling co-existed with wild inconsistency, so that generalisation about scribal practice is impossible. In the early part of the period, we have on the one hand the liberal attitude of the Peterborough annalist, with his multiple variants, and on the other the neurotic consistency of Orm, whose written language deviates from his spoken language in the cause of consistency to the extent of excising certain words and morphemes which must in fact have formed part of the ordinary variation in his everyday speech.[8]

Among the scribes of Chaucer manuscripts similar variation in attitude is found between individuals. A rare window is opened upon scribal attitudes by Scribe A of MS Gg.4.27, who repeatedly duplicates material he is copying (CT.B[1], 981–7; CT.B[2], 3006–16; TC.I, 582–95 and II, 1233–39), and on each occasion his duplicated passages differ from one another not merely in spelling alone, but morphologically and lexically also. The variation between the two copyings exhibits the ubiquitous fluctuation between *i* and *y*, between capitalised and lower-case graphs, between abbreviations and words written out in full. Setting these aside, however, there remain forty-seven instances in which there are further discrepancies between his two copyings. Indeed, the changes imposed in the second copying may be substantial, such as the apparent interpolation of phrases, the use of different words —*eyper* rather than *euere*; *and* rather than *or*; *seyde* rather than *qud*; *oftyn* rather than *ful ofte*—and changes in the tense of the verb —*wepede* becomes *wepith*; or they may be merely alterations in spelling: *retorne/returne*, *rewthe/reuthe*, *peyne/payne*, *god/good*, *wel/weel*. Most striking of all is that, even within one of the renderings of a passage, the scribe is not consistent in his spelling, thus *gret(e)* and *greet*; *agylt* and *agilt*, *trespas* and *trespace*, *hye* and *highe* occur as alternatives within a few lines of one another, the last of these corresponding with *heye* in the first copying. Some of this variation is perhaps the result of forms constrained by his exemplar, but other forms have certainly been imposed by the scribe himself without regard for consistency.

In their introduction to the facsimile of this manuscript, Malcolm Parkes and Richard Beadle raise an interesting question of the aesthetics of text presentation when they point out that when the passage from *Troilus and Criseyde* was recopied variants were used in rhyme without much regard for creating matching pairs of spellings.[9] Indeed, although the second copying twice (in the cases of *lyf* and *lyue* and *rewthe* and *reuthe*) creates eye-rhyme missing in the first copying, in three other cases (*Crisseyde/Cresseide*; *fly3t/flyth*; *peyne/payne*) the alteration destroys existing eye-rhyme. The treatment of spellings in rhyme is of especial interest, since it is in this position if anywhere that a copyist's attention should be most forcibly drawn to the correspondence between sound and spelling. But the implication of Parkes and Beadle's remarks is that this is not a purely linguistic matter, for scribes may reasonably be expected to have been attracted by the visual matching of line ends as part of the *ordinatio* of a verse text. Indeed, scribes who elsewhere translate the spellings of words whilst recopying will often preserve the rhymes of the original even if they are dialectally heterogeneous.[10] The extent to which they did this was of course variable, and, as well as being prompted by simple visual matching, would certainly have been influenced by the prevailing literary aesthetic with regard to rhyme. It is clear, for example, that in earlier Middle English, half-rhyme and assonance were aesthetically acceptable, and that this is reflected in mismatches of spellings in rhyme.[11] Although the reflection in orthography of this literary aesthetic may in principle be distinguished from that lack of eye-rhyme which arose simply from a failure in orthographic consistency, the contemporary reader is unlikely to have regularly recognised this distinction in practice. Both kinds of mismatch are found in the popular London romances of the generation before Chaucer. But Chaucer himself seems to have been peculiarly concerned with purity in rhyme, and it may seem natural for the spellings in Chaucer manuscripts to have reflected this concern. In fact, among the extant manuscripts, there is considerable variation in practice, even though it is evident that the variants available to most scribes offered them the opportunity, should they wish to take it, of emphasising pure rhyme by means of matching spellings, even if these had not been found in the exemplar. An increased tendency to emphasise pure rhyme by spelling choice was an aesthetic act, both visual and auditory, motivated on one hand by a concern for the visual effect of page layout, but on the other by a regard for stabilised spelling and the consistent representation of a phoneme by the appropriate grapheme.

The point has recently been made by Vance Ramsey that the scribe (or, as he argues, scribes) who wrote the Ellesmere and Hengwrt manuscripts showed particular care in avoiding brevigraphs at the line end.[12] It is a sensitivity to this position which is paralleled by the spelling of rhymes in these two manuscripts. Figures for the failure of eye-rhyme in selected passages from some of the earlier Chaucer manuscripts are given in table 1. Figures in parenthesis refer to mismatches due to proper nouns, traditional spellings of pronouns, and the verb form *is*. It is at once apparent that Parkes and Doyle's Scribe B habitually writes eye-rhymes to a far greater degree than any other scribe examined, or indeed than Caxton's compositor. Some other features of this performance are also worthy of note: firstly, the quality

Table 1

	Hg	El	Gg.4.27	H7334	Cp198	Caxton 1484	Dd.4.24
GP	26 (9)	26 (9)	58 (5)	59 (6)	57 (10)	58 (14)	——
WBProl+T	77 (39)	59 (33)	99 (17)	96 (17)	130 (24)	103 (16)	130 (29)
MLProl+T	58 (16)	39 (16)	90 (9)	97 (24)	115 (20)	111 (14)	——
Totals	161 (64)	124 (58)	247 (31)	252 (47)	302 (54)	272 (44)	——

Note: In cases where manuscripts are lacking lines by comparison with the texts of El and Hg, lines have been substituted to achieve comparable numbers: in the case of GP from MiT; MLT from ClT, and WBProl+T from FriT.

of the rhyme spellings, where a high proportion of failures to match rhyme in spellings arises from the use of proper nouns, the traditional spellings of pronouns, and also those of the type represented in rhymes like *Philosophre* : *cofre* and *savith* : *significavit*. This makes the distinction between El and Hg and the other texts even more pronounced. Further, El can be seen to represent a distinct advance on Hg in terms of the matching of spellings in rhyme. Not only is there a tendency to match rhymes even more carefully, but the proportion of failures to do so which arise from observance of traditional spellings is higher still than in Hg. It is as thought the scribe is attracted by two competing kinds of consistency, that of the spelling tradition and that of the aesthetics of rhyme.

El is, of course, an expensively produced and prestigious manuscript, and it cannot be that the increase in the incidence of matching spellings there is merely coincidental. The only other example of Chaucerian copying attributed to this scribe, the Hatfield House fragment of *Troilus and Criseyde*, similarly shows a breach of eye-rhyme running at half the rate of another carefully copied *Troilus* manuscript, Corpus Christi College, Cambridge MS. 61. The presence of this concern with eye-rhyme in manuscripts associated with the work of a single scribe suggests that we are dealing with an aspect of that scribe's performance rather than with a practice inherited through his exemplars from the poet. This impression is further borne out by the fact that the failure to write eye-rhyme at any particular point correlates only loosely with what is written in other manuscripts. This being so, what is the significance of this practice? If scribe B had been fully conscious of the importance of matching spellings either as an aesthetic effect of the *ordinatio* or a part of the linguistic art of orthography, and if he had allotted high priority to such considerations, we might have expected him to have achieved a higher level of correct eye-rhymes than he in fact does. Clearly it was not a conscious priority. Nevertheless, there seems to have been a tendency in his practice—emphasised when he was copying most carefully—to adopt a kind of consistency within the specific environment of rhymed words, a tendency to emphasise the correspondence between phonic and written modes of language, which was balanced in him by another kind of consistency, a regard for logographic norms of spelling in the case of certain words. Too much should not be made of this in relation to standardisation, but it can reasonably be argued that here we find a professional writer whose practice shows a kind of orderliness of mind with regard to his profession, and in those areas where it is necessary for the formation of a consistent writing system. To a higher degree than usual, and perhaps in part motivated by literary-aesthetic considerations, he was ready to make a selection from the repertoire of his forms in a way which suggests that he might have been sympathetic to the development of a standardised writing system.

Within a few years of the date at which the Ellesmere manuscript must have been written, a similar orderliness of mind is exhibited by the compiler of a concordance of the Wycliffite Bible.[13] His method was rigorously alphabetical, but variation in spelling practice caused him difficulties of which he was well aware. Uncomplainingly, he explains the need to look up the variant forms ȝift and *gift*, *kirke* and *chirche*, *epistle* and *pistle*. Some, he notes, use the symbol *yogh*, others *g*; some þ, others *th*; some write initial *h*, others omit it. Consequently, divergence between his own practice and that of the user of his concordance is foreseen, and the resulting disorganisation warned against:

aftir my manere of writyng, sum word stondiþ in sum place, which same word, aftir þi maner of writyng, shulde stonde in anoþir place.

Rather than fretting about the fate of his labour at the hands of copyists, he is pleasantly encouraging to those who wish to adapt the work to their own tastes:

> If it plese to ony man to write þis concordaunce, & him þenkiþ þat summe wordis ben not set in ordre after his conseit & his manere of writyng, it is not hard, if he take keep wiþ good avisement in his owne writyng, to sette suche wordis in such an ordre as his owne conseit accordiþ wel to.

If he is reasonably careful and works systematically, the compiler seems to be saying, the concordance can be transformed into a configuration which will suit each user. Conscientious and orderly industry is being proffered as an alternative to standardisation. This quietist and frankly unworldly solution to the problem of variation contrasts markedly with the tone of complaint which echoes through most early references to the English language.

Although no one in the medieval period, much less any copyist of Chaucerian manuscripts, made specific suggestions for its standardisation, commentary upon the English language is by no means lacking. This commentary falls, more or less, into three categories: that concerned with the problems of translation into English (this dates largely from the fifteenth century); that concerned with the rivalry of English and French in England (which has been discontinued by the fifteenth century); and disapproving commentary on the diversity of the English language (this spans the entire period).

The diversity of vernacular languages at the lexical as well as the orthographical level was a well-recognised phenomenon in medieval times. In the thirteenth century, Roger Bacon makes a distinction in his *Greek Grammar* between language and dialect, defining the latter as those usages which are particular to certain sub-groups among the speakers of the language.[14] Greek had its dialects; so too does medieval Latin:

In lingua enim latina que vna est, sunt multa idiomata. Substancia enim ipsius lingue consistit in hijs in quibus communicant clerici et literati omnes. Idiomata vero sunt multa secundum multitudinem nacionum vtencium hac lingua. Quia aliter in multis pronunciant et scribunt ytalici, et aliter hyspani, et aliter gallici, et aliter teutonici, et aliter anglici et ceteri. (Dist.I, cap.i)

Here, and also in his *Opus tertium* and *Compendium studii philosophiae*, Bacon discusses the dialects of French and mentions those of the north, south, east, and west of England. Diversity in dialect, he says, leads to social ridicule: "manifeste videmus quod aliquid optime et proprie sonat in uno idiomate et ridiculose sonat in alio; ut patet non solum de longinquis sed propinquissimis; sicut de Picardis et Gallicis; nam mutuo se derident" (*Opus tertium*, XV), and also to problems of stylistic choice, as Caxton noted many years later.

Linguistic antipathy between the speakers of neighbouring dialects may manifest itself in deliberate alterations to manuscripts[15] or in that inadvertent scribal corruption of texts feared by both Robert Mannyng and Chaucer, but it also emerges openly in the plots of fabliaux and other works of fiction as mockery. In the French tale of the *Dous anglois et de l'anel* the defective French of two Englishmen leads to misadventure when they confuse the pronunciation of the word for "lamb" with that for "ass." It is important to realise, however, that the tale is not simply anti-English, for it also contains a passing shot at another stigmatised variety of French, the language of the Auvergne. This, then, is rather an assertion of *francien* against provincial forms of French than Gallic chauvinism, and as such it is parallel with the experience of the Picard poet, Conon de Béthune, who, when he visited the French court, like the English heroine of *Jehan et Blonde*, had to endure criticism of his accent, expressed in the adage that he had "not been born at Pontoise." By the mid-thirteenth century, French of the Paris area was well on the road to becoming a standard, or at least was being forcefully promoted as such.

In England, in the late fourteenth century, matters had not yet progressed so far. Dialectal solidarity against the outsider furnishes some of the fun of the Reeve's Tale and, as Cecily Clark

notes, attitudes to linguistic diversity could also lead to the perse-
cution of individuals from outside the dialect area.[16] There may,
it is true, be some implicit acceptance of the primacy of southern English in the Wakefield Second Shepherds' play, but this
attitude is based as much on the French lexis in the speech as
the southern dialectal forms. In any case, finding common cause
against speakers of another dialect scarcely constitutes evidence
of the desire for a standard. Indeed, as Bacon noted, it is not in
popular linguistic antipathies but among the usage of clerks and
scholars that the attitudes which may promote a standard should
be sought. What concerned scholars with regard to English was
its corruption.

Corruption of the text by scribal copying was a well-recognised
phenomenon in medieval commentary; but this notion of corruption is extendable to the language also. Indeed, the opposition
between purity and corruption as states of the language itself goes
back in English linguistic history at least to Giraldus Cambrensis,
who, in the 1190s, in his *Description of Wales*, considered the
language of Devon to represent the purest English. The remainder
of the country, he thought, had had its linguistic resources corrupted by contact with Danes and Norwegians. A similar idea,
with naturally a different perspective, is to be found much later in
Osbern Bokenham's *Mappula Angliae* (c.1440), which expands
Ranulph Higden's commentary on the languages of Britain in his
Polichronicon. In Bokenham's view the barbarians who have corrupted English are now the Scots, but French too has played its
part. An attempt by ordinary people to master French for the
sake of career advantage has meant that "by processe of tyme
barbariȝid thei in bothyn and spekyne neythyr good ffrensch nor
good Englyssh." *MED*, which records only Bokenham's use of
the word *barbariȝid*, glosses it as "to speak corruptly or barba-
rously." Yet, in this context there is no doubt that corruption arose
in Bokenham's opinion through the adoption by each language of
words and forms proper to the other. Indeed, his additions to Higden revolve around this notion of the contamination of pure Saxon
by foreign influence, and he commences by the statement that
England "haþe dyuersites of toungis and languagis. Nerþelees

they been not alle pure, but sum ben mixte and medlid on sundry ways." Although the Scots and Welsh retain their pure original tongues, for English we have a theory of linguistic evolution by contamination.

The language used to present this view (*corrupt, barbariʒid, pure*) is relatively technical and has its counterpart in Latin teachings concerning the writing of a correct style. The use of the word *barbariʒid* is therefore not simply a gratuitous insult. It is used with technical appropriateness to refer to the importation of undesirable foreign words and phrases which detracted from polished writing. The fact that Bokenham is here applying to English the aesthetic judgements appropriate to Latin composition is worth investigating further.

According to the *Rhetorica ad Herennium* good style hung upon three points: *elegantia*, which derived from *Latinitas* and *explanatio* (clarity); *conpositio* (mellifluous composition); and *dignitas*, which derived from the skilled use of figurative language. The latter two, *conpositio* and *dignitas*, were at least in principle attemptable in vernacular languages, and there is no reason why English authors, like those in France, should not have sought to achieve euphony and to dignify their discourse with the devices of rhetoric. But the pursuit of an English analogue to *elegantia* was more problematic, for although the precepts for clarity of diction were readily observable, no easy equivalent for *Latinitas* could be found in English. This is because *Latinitas* entails that uniformity of language which Bacon saw in Latin superordinate to the diversity among its users. The *Ad Herennium* defines Latinity as the avoidance of soloecism and of barbarism, and this standard definition is echoed by Chirius Fortunatianus, who considers it to arise from lexico-grammatical congruity and the avoidance of barbarism. Such typical definitions of the basic essentials of good style presuppose a circumstance notably lacking in English: an agreed standard of what, among a readership of educated men, constituted acceptable grammar and diction.

Yet medieval awareness of the possibility of vernacular standards is already implicit in Bacon's reference to *purum Gallicum* in contradistinction to other dialects of French, and also in the use by one Alanus, a twelfth-century commentator on the *Ad Herennium*, quoted by Harry Caplan, of a vernacular example to illustrate the significance of the term *Latinitas*: "thus Gallicum is said to be pure when Normanisms do not intrude."[17] Moreover, Constance's use in the Man of Law's Tale of *a maner Latyn corrupt* presupposes, as John Burrow has shown, a particular conception of language history.[18] Post-Imperial Latin was said by Isidore and by Vincent of Beauvais to have been corrupted "per soloecismos et barbarismos," and indeed literate men in Chaucer's time could still regard contemporary Italian as no more than corrupt Latin: "the comoun puple in Italie spekith Latyn corrupt, as trewe men seyn, that han ben in Italie."[19] *MED*'s citations for "corruption" and "corruptly" confirm this association of the word with language history. Bokenham's allegation, therefore, that English had been corrupted by foreign influences, carries with it a well-recognised assumption that contemporary vernacular languages, although now debased and diversified, must once have existed in a pure and undivided state. Why then did medieval English authors, unlike their neighbours in France, show so little interest in the establishment of a new English standard? Why indeed did a man born in England, a scholar like Roger Bacon, show more interest in the relation of French dialects to a standard than any similar relationship in his mother tongue? The answer is, of course, that throughout the thirteenth and fourteenth centuries England did indeed possess a standard written language, but paradoxically that language was a form of French.[20] The situation in England was one of diglossia, in which the superordinate language bore no dialectal relation to the demotic, and the latter was of little interest to literate people. Only when they were compelled to discontinue the use of French did they find it necessary to consider the shortcomings of English. With the more extended use of English and the alienation of French, we find Bokenham lamenting the barbarisation by contact with French in much the same way as Giraldus Cambrensis had earlier decried its barbarisation by the Scandinavian languages.

These expressed attitudes emphasise the fact that standardisation in its broader sense has always been an ambiguous concept, viewable both from descriptive linguistic and also from evaluative socio-stylistic perspectives which often masquerade as aesthetic judgements. In descriptive linguistic terms, the Scandinavian contribution to English had in fact encouraged standardisation as much as promoted diversification, since terms like *they*, *get*, *fellow*, and so on, were used widely throughout the country. In general, however, Scandinavian terms were not perceived as especially elevated or desirable components of literary diction. The position of French however was very different, since as a superordinate standard vernacular it offered not only wide and relatively consistent use, but also social prestige. Whilst it continued to occupy a position of esteem, before changes in attitude saw it as a source of barbarism, it was a source of supra-dialectal lexis which was at once acceptable socially and defensible artistically.

For those who saw stylistic ideals through the lenses of Latin literacy, Horace justified the borrowing of words from a culturally admired source, and Chirius Fortunatianus gave precise directions on the cultivation of a worthy vocabulary. His is a strategy of seek and avoid. To be avoided are *verba obsoleta* and *vulgaria*, the language of uneducated men, démodé diction and clichés; *obscura*, hard words known only to a few scholars; *aliena*, words not suited to the purpose or genre of the discourse; and *gentilia*, words of provincial or *déclassé* origin. To be sought out are *verba splendida*, multi-syllabic words of euphonious quality; *antiqua*, old words of established literary connotation; *propria*, technically appropriate words; and *translata*, metaphorical usages. As Roger Bacon, and after him George Zipf, remarked, in English the common everyday words are often monosyllabic;[21] words of technical discourse and less frequent occurrence are polysyllabic. Thus, the choice for any medieval author who set himself to adapt the Latin ideals of style to English was clear enough: it was in the Romance languages that he must seek distinguished diction. Mendenhall long ago made the connection between Fortunatianus's precepts and aureate diction, but the process need not be expressed so narrowly.[22] Stylistically motivated adoption from French and Francified Latin was a continuous process throughout the Middle Ages. Possessing both social prestige and artistic justification, the importation of French words and phrases into English represents a force for standardisation, not by the extension of dialect usage but to a considerable extent by the broadening of a technical style into more general use.

Let us now return to the matter of Chancery Standard. This, we may recall, was a relatively consistent spelling system associated with an important office of state. Documents written in this orthography, and written in a characteristic script, were further marked by a distinctive manner of textual coherence proper to legal and administrative language, which has become known as the "curial style."[23] The syntactic and cohesive patterns of curial style emerged first in Latin but were developed relatively independently in the French used widely for administrative matters. For authors seeking a mode of expression which bore the cachet of association with important men and the business of state, the mannered structures of curial style with its frequently Romance diction offered a readily imitated and prestigious model. It was used by the authors especially in prologues and epilogues, where elevated style was most necessary, but adapted also for narrative purposes in romance and chronicle.[24] We are today accustomed to regard verse as superior to prose, but something of the value placed on artful prose at the beginning of the fifteenth century can be gauged from Christine de Pizan's words (*Le Dit de la Rose*, 573–78) in describing the golden letter instituting her Order of the Rose: written with the letters carefully formed in azure, "non pas rimées/ Ne furent, mais en belle prose."[25] Both in England and in France the authors of prose were affected directly by the curial style of official documents. From the English perspective in the fifteenth century, however, this style derived further esteem by its association with French, the language of cultural prestige in medieval England. Any tendency to adapt the domestic Anglo-French curial style to literary purposes was greatly reinforced by the practice of translating prose romances from French; romances whose style was often itself an adaptation of the curial style written in the chancelleries of France and Burgundy.

The standardisation of the written language which took place during the fifteenth century was in part the product of the organisation of a department of government to write its documents in a relatively consistent form of English to replace the French "standard" to which it had hitherto adhered. The extension of that standard to non-administrative writing seems at least to have been facilitated by the identification of a common feature of the style of administrative documents as desirable in lending elevation to English literary style. All this took place against a background in which medieval scholars were aware of the division between dialects and the prestige standard language, and clearly felt the deficiency of English as a literary medium through its lack of such standardisation. Thus the Chancery spelling system became available to a world which was perfectly capable of appreciating its benefits in terms purely of communicative efficiency; but it was also associated with a type of style which was socially and aesthetically admirable. By its association with this style, its spelling norms seem to have been more readily extensible from the narrow register of its original use to the broader one of literary use. In most significant changes to the language, the mechanical linguistic processes, the purely structural and communicative advantages, must be reinforced by the motivation of social approval for the change to become fully effective. In no case is this more true than in the standardisation of late medieval English.

NOTES

1. E. Ekwall, *Studies on the Population of Medieval London* (Stockholm: Almqvist and Wiksell, 1956).

2. Malcolm Richardson, "Henry V, the English Chancery, and Chancery English," *Speculum* 55 (1980):726–50.

3. M. L. Samuels, "Some Applications of Middle English Dialectology," *ES* 44 (1963):81–94.

4. Jeremy Smith has drawn attention to the way in which copyists were able to recognise and reproduce characteristic features of Gower's orthography. Jeremy J. Smith, "Linguistic Features of Some Fifteenth-Century Middle English Manuscripts" in *Manuscripts and Readers in Fifteenth-Century England*, edited by Derek Pearsall (Cambridge: D. S. Brewer, 1983), 104–12.

5. In addition to works mentioned above, the following may be cited among recent scholarship: John H. Fisher, Malcolm Richardson, and Jane L. Fisher, *An Anthology of Chancery English* (Knoxville: University of Tennessee Press, 1984); John H. Fisher, "Chancery Standard and Modern Written English," *Journal of the Society of Archivists* 6 (1979): 136–44; Michael Benskin, "Local Archives and Middle English Dialects," *Journal of the Society of Archivists* 5 (1977):500–14. The sociolinguistic perspective on standardisation is emphasised by Arthur O. Sandved, "Prologemona to a Renewed Study of the Use of Standard English," in *So Meny People, Longages and Tonges: Philological Essays in Scots and Medieval English presented to Angus McIntosh*, edited by Michael Benskin and M. L. Samuels (Edinburgh: privately published, 1981), 31–42; and for a discussion of Chancery Standard in comparison with other fifteenth-century types, see, in the same collection, M. L. Samuels, "Spelling and Dialect in the Late and Post-Middle English Periods," (43–54).

6. R. Vance Ramsey, "Paleography and Scribes of Shared Training," *Studies in the Age of Chaucer* 8 (1986):107–14.

7. The most detailed account of scribal translation now available is that by Michael Benskin and Margaret Laing, "Translations and *Mischsprachen* in Middle English Manuscripts," in Benskin and Samuels, *So Meny People*.

8. R. W. Burchfield, "The Language and Orthography of the *Ormulum* Manuscript," *Transactions of the Philological Society* (1956):56–87.

9. M. B. Parkes and R. Beadle, Introduction to *The Poetical Works of Geoffrey Chaucer: A Facsimile of Cambridge University Library MS Gg.4.27*, 3 vols. (Cambridge: D. S. Brewer, 1979–80), vol. 3, p. 51.

10. Indeed Maldwyn Mills argues that Thomas Chestre was prepared to use pronunciations alien to his dialect to achieve smooth rhymes. *Lybeaus Desconus*, edited by Maldwyn Mills, Early English Text Society OS 261 (1969), 34–36.

11. This tradition of half-rhyme is mentioned by Angus McIntosh, "Early Middle English Alliterative Verse" in *Middle English Alliterative Poetry and its Literary Background*, edited by David Lawton (Cambridge: D. S. Brewer, 1982), 20–33.

12. The scribe is given the sigil B by A. I. Doyle and M. B. Parkes in "The Production of Copies of the *Canterbury Tales* and the *Confessio Amantis* in the Early Fifteenth Century" in *Medieval Scribes, Manuscripts and Libraries: Essays presented to N. R. Ker*, edited by M. B. Parkes and A. G. Watson (London: Scolar Press, 1978), 163–210. His

identification as a single scribe had, however, been made much earlier. A bibliography of the debate may be found in Vance Ramsey's "Paleography and Scribes of Shared Training."

13. Most recently edited by Sherman M. Kuhn, "The Preface to a Fifteenth-Century Concordance," *Speculum* 43 (1968):258–73.

14. *The Greek Grammar of Roger Bacon*, edited by Edmond Nolan and S. A. Hirsch (Cambridge: Cambridge University Press, 1902); Rogeri Baconi, *Opera Quaedam Hactena Inedita*, Rolls Series IV.15 (1859), 90, 438, 467. For a recent treatment of learned concern with the vernacular in the Middle Ages, see Serge Lusignan, *Parler Vulgairement: Les Intellectuels et la Langue française aux xiii^e et xiv^e siecles* (Paris and Montreal, 1986).

15. Thomas G. Duncan, "A Middle English Linguistic Reviser," *Neuphilologische Mitteilungen* 82 (1981):162–74. See also Smith, "Linguistic Features," for a further example of dialectal censorship.

16. A witness born in Scotland was deemed untrustworthy by a York magistrate in 1364 because of the instability of his dialect pronunciation. Cecily Clark, "Another Late-Fourteenth-Century Case of Dialect-Awareness," *English Studies* 62 (1981):504–5.

17. Harry Caplan, *Of Eloquence: Studies in Ancient and Medieval Rhetoric*, edited by Anne King and Helen North (Ithaca, N.Y.: Cornell University Press, 1970), 269–70.

18. J. Burrow, "A Maner Latyn Corrupt," *Medium Ævum* 30 (1961): 33–37.

19. *The Holy Bible, by John Wycliffe and his followers*, edited by J. Forshall and F. Madden (London, 1850), 59. Also quoted is a tract from CUL MS Ii.6.26 which argues the need for scriptures in national languages: "to Frensshe men bokis of Frensche, to Ytaliens bokis of Latyne corrupte . . ." (xiv).

20. W. Rothwell, "Stratford atte Bowe and Paris," *Modern Language Review* 80 (1985):39–54.

21. George K. Zipf, *The Psycho-Biology of Language: An Introduction to Dynamic Philology* (1935; reprint, Cambridge, Mass: MIT Press, 1965), 20–28.

22. J. C. Mendenhall, *Aureate Terms: A Study in the Literary Diction of the Fifteenth Century* (Lancaster, Pa.: Wickersham Printing Co., 1919).

23. Jens Rasmussen, *La prose narrative française du XVe siecle* Copenhagen: Munksgaard, 1958), 32.

24. J. D. Burnley, "Curial Prose in England," *Speculum* 61 (1986),

593–614. With different emphases, a similar connection between the administrative style of Chancery and contemporary literature is also made by Malcolm Richardson in "The *Dictamen* and Its Influence on Fifteenth-Century English Prose," *Rhetorica* 2 (1984):207–26, in J. H. Fisher's "Chaucer and the Written Language," in *The Popular Literature of Medieval England*, edited by Thomas J. Heffernan, Tennessee Studies in Literature 28 (Knoxville: University of Tennessee Press, 1985), 237–51, and also in his "Caxton and Chancery English," in *Fifteenth-Century Studies: Recent Essays*, edited by R. F. Yeager (New York: Archon, 1984).

25. *Oeuvres poétiques de Christine de Pisan*, edited by Maurice Roy, 3 vols, SATF (Paris, 1886–96), vol. 2, p. 46.

Standards from the Past: The Conservative Syllable Structure of the Alliterative Revival

Thomas Cable

PHONOLOGY, REGISTER, TRADITION

With reference to both Chaucer and Langland, M. L. Samuels has made the point that "in the late xiv century in southern England the use of *-e* depended on varying conditions of stress and register, and the individual usage of an author cannot be established simply on the evidence of when and where he lived."[1] My own study of fourteenth-century meter and phonology has reached the conclusion that final *-e* was alive generally in the poems of the Alliterative Revival, not just in *Piers Plowman*. The evidence points, in Samuels' terms, to a conservative register for the composition of these poems. The idea of various registers of formality and conservatism makes my conclusion less sweepingly contradictory of familiar statements than it might otherwise seem. Traditional grammars and handbooks refer to the loss of final *-e* in the West Midlands at this time, and doubtless there were varieties of the language (according to locality, time, individual speaker, and register) in which the syllable was lost.[2] However, I shall argue that the *Gawain*-poet and the other major poets of the Revival made use of systematic final *-e* throughout the composition of their alliterative long lines.

The focus of the present essay will be quite specific: an account of the final syllables of the words at the ends of the lines in *Cleanness*. However, the conclusion can be generalized to the ends of lines in other poems, including *Sir Gawain and the Green Knight*, *Piers Plowman*, *Morte Arthure*, *The Parlement of the Thre Ages*, *William of Palerne*, *Alexander A*, and *The Wars of Alexander*.

More importantly, it will become evident that what is involved is not simply inflectional *-e* but also the phonological shape of the whole word at an earlier stage, whether from Old English, Old French, or Old Norse. Finally, the conclusion about the syllable at the end of the line holds the key to an understanding of the interacting principles of rhythm in the poetry as a whole.

The results that I come to are somewhat different from those of Marie Borroff, who recognizes the use of final *-e* in some of the wheels of *Gawain*, leaves open the possibility of final *-e* at the end of the long line, and disallows it within the long line.[3] It is true, as Borroff points out, that the long lines and the wheels derive from two different traditions. Of final *-e* in the wheels she writes, "Its sporadic sounding is thus warranted by principles of rhyme and meter, and analogous principles must be established to warrant its sounding in the long alliterative lines" (171). What follows is an attempt to establish some of those principles. The results suggest that the poet's phonological rules move easily between the two metrical traditions. As Angus McIntosh has pointed out, the main metrical categories that we impose on medieval poetry (alliterative vs. rhyming, accentual vs. syllabic, even prose vs. poetry) are modern polar terms that are often more misleading than helpful (although they can be helpful if they are taken to indicate roughly the line of a spectrum).[4]

John Fisher has shown that many of the forms of modern written English "originated as the conscious or unconscious choices of a handful of men in a strategic position at the moment of the creation of the official language."[5] If the clerks of Chancery between 1420 and 1460 were shaping the English language as it was to be, it is interesting to contemplate that a handful of poets a century earlier had already preserved, as though in amber, the English language as it had been.

OLD NORSE LOANS

The discussion that follows draws on a complete scansion and grammatical parsing of all 1,812 lines in *Cleanness*.[6] The analysis includes the etymology of every word in the poem and a marking of every syllable that would have occurred historically—as the word would have appeared in Old English, Old French, Old Norse, or Latin (the last category consisting mainly of a few Biblical names). This text, which I have analyzed and reanalyzed several times through, is part of a larger, similarly treated corpus of 6,100 long lines of Middle English alliterative poetry.

The distribution in *Cleanness* of loans from Old Norse is striking. Of the 3,624 hemistichs in the poem, 179 end with words borrowed into Middle English from Old Norse: 97 at the end of the a-verse, 82 at the end of the b-verse. The occurrences of the Old Norse loans at the end of the a-verse are split about equally between words that ended in a stressed syllable in Old Norse (52 instances) and those that ended in an unstressed syllable (45 instances); thus:

(1)

533a   Wylde wormeȝ to her won   (< ON van)

1259a   Boþe to cayre at þe kart   (< ON kartr)

569a   Þat ilke skyl for no scaþe   (< ON skaði)

767a   And Godde glydeȝ his gate   (< ON gate)

By contrast, 74 of the 82 occurrences of Old Norse loans in the b-verse ended with an unstressed syllable that reflects a historical syllable in Old Norse:

(2)

59b   ryȝt to þe sete   (< ON sæti)

469b   and setteȝ on þe doue   (< ON dufa)

The remaining eight verses ended in one of three words that did not have a final unstressed syllable in Old Norse: the postponed preposition *tylle* (882b, 1064b, 1174b, 1752b), the adverbs *þertylle* (1509b) and *are* (438b, 1128b), and the noun *scole* (1145b).

These facts require an explanation. Why is it that a-verses end freely in words that had a final consonant in Old Norse? These words include *won* (ON *van*), *tolke* (ON *tulkr*), *glam* (ON *glamm*), *layk* (ON *leikr*), *dam* (ON *dammr*), *karle* (ON *karl*), *brest* (ON *brestr*), *ryfte* (ON *ript*), *skwe* (ON *sky*), *syt* (ON **syt*), *ȝarm*

(ON *jarmr*), *flot* (ON *flot*), *kest* (ON *kast*), *tom* (ON *tom*), *kart* (ON *kartr*), *unþryfte* (ON *þrift*), *scylle* (ON *skil*), *cal* noun (ON *kall*), *walt* (ON *val*), *wyȝt* (ON *vigt*), *skelt* (?ON *skellt*), *þro* (ON *þrar*), *aloȝ* (*a* + ON *lagr*), and *bayn* (ON *beinn*). Yet none of these monosyllabic words appears at the end of the b-verse in *Cleanness*. In the b-verse the only final Old Norse loans that were originally monosyllabic are a recurring preposition; two adverbs, which could have acquired an analogical *-e*, as adverbs often did; and the noun *scole*.

My own explanation is to treat *tylle*, *are*, and *scole* as exceptional (either in their phonological development or in their metrical usage) and to hypothesize three general principles:

(3)
(i)   The second half-line must end on an unstressed syllable.
(ii) Old Norse loans that ended in a final vowel retain that vowel as *-e* in the language of this fourteenth-century text.
(iii) Nouns from Old Norse do not have an inflectional syllable in the dative case.

The point about the dative in (3.iii) is to limit the generalization in (3.ii) and explain why objects of prepositions account for a substantial proportion of the loans in both halves of the line. But in the a-verse, 20 of the singular prepositional objects ended in a consonant in the nominative singular in Old Norse, as in the first two examples in (1). In the b-verse, all seven singular prepositional objects ended in a vowel, as in the examples in (2). A logical conclusion to draw is that those nouns that had a final vowel in the nominative singular retained it in all cases in this text, and those that did not have one did not add a vowel for the dative.

When faced with what C. S. Peirce calls "surprising facts" (here the distribution of Old Norse loans in the two halves of the line), the idea is to develop a general explanation from which the facts would follow as a matter of course.[7] The results of this hypothesized explanation, the formation of which Peirce terms "abduction," can then be tested inductively. The three-part hypothesis in (3) is fairly general and complete except for a couple of ragged edges: an analogical -*e* must be assumed for two adverbs, and *scole* is simply an exception. However, the hypothesis can be accepted until a simpler and more general explanation is proposed. Such is the usual progress in paradigms of science. (The only other critical response is to show that the surprising facts are not surprising after all.)

As it turns out, the hypothesis in (3) gains support from the much larger group of Old French loans. When both sets of loanwords are added to the still larger group of native English words at the end of verses, we can discern several pervasive principles of phonology and meter running through these texts.

OLD FRENCH LOANS

In the 1,812 lines of *Cleanness* there are 661 Old French loans at the ends of half-lines, 420 in the first half-line and 241 in the second. For example:

(4)

39a   Þen þe harlot with haste   (< OF haste)

970b   þat no wyȝe achaped   (< OF achaper)

1393b   watȝ towched of þe feste   (< OF feste)

Of the 420 words at the end of the first half-line, 72 were monosyllabic or ended in a stressed syllable in Old French (or Anglo-Norman) and would not have had a final -*e* historically. For example:

(5)

17a   He is so clene in his courte   (< OF court)

245a   Þe defence watȝ þe fryt   (< OF fruit)

1199a   And þay stoken so strayt   (< OF estreit)

By contrast, only nine b-verses end in Old French loans that would be read as monosyllabic.[8] What do not occur at the end of the b-verse are the numerous monosyllabic words that end the a-verse: *courte* (OF *cort*), *prys* (OF *pris*), *duk* (OF *duc*), *fryt* (OF *fruit*), *fayth* (OF *feid*), *soun* (OF *son*), *bost* (OF *bost*), *fol* (OF *fol*), *dece* (OF *deis*), *trot* (OF *trot*), *fete* (OF *fet*), *oste* (OF *ost*), *cry* noun (OF *cri*), *scorne* (OF *escarn*), *clos* (OF *clos*), *beke* (OF *bec*), *gyn* (OF *engin*), *grece* (OF *grez*), *gaye* (OF *gai*), *playn* (OF *plain*), *false* (OF *fals*), *fers* (OF *fers*), *chef* (OF *chef*), and *strayt* (OF *estreit*).

Again, these facts require an explanation in any theory of Middle English phonology and meter. Principles similar to those that I hypothesized for the Old Norse loans account for the conservative syllabic structure of words borrowed from Old French. A fairly detailed statement of the principles appears in (6) below. However, it is the overall system that I wish to make clear at this point, and that system can best be seen by proceeding directly to the group of native English words.

NATIVE WORDS

The distribution of syllabic patterns in loanwords at the ends of first and second half-lines has provided insights into phonology and meter at once. Now we come to the largest group of verses classified according to the final word—those ending in words descending from Old English. Here we have compelling evidence that historical final -*e* was an essential factor in the meter, and we can be quite specific. For example, a large number of the discriminations depended on a classification of nouns according to their grammatical gender.

By my count, 450, or 25 percent, of the first half-lines in *Cleanness* end with a stressed syllable in a native English word. Only 27, or 1.5 percent, of the second half-lines end with such a stressed syllable by my understanding of the grammatical principles as applied to the extant text. Of the words at the end of the first half-line, a large number are monosyllabic masculine and neuter objects of prepositions; there are almost no occurrences of this category at the end of the second half-line—words such as *folk* (OE *folc*, n.), *dom* (OE *dom*, m.), *hous* (OE *hus*, n.), *wyf* (OE *wif*, n.), *wind* (OE *wind*, m.), *worde* (OE *word*, n.), *wyt* (OE *witt*, n.), *craft* (OE *cræft*, m.), *blod* (OE *blod*, n.), *ston* (OE *stan*, m.), *flesch* (OE *flæsc*, n.), *clop* (OE *clap*, m.), *bour* (OE *bur*, n.), *bak* (OE *bæc*, n.), *font* (OE *font*, m.), *mode* (OE *mod*, n.), *londe* (OE *land*, n.), *werk* (OE *weorc*, n.), *glem* (OE *glæm*, m.), *storme* (OE *storm*, m.), *clay* (OE *clæg*, m.), *wryt* (OE *writ*, n.), and dozens more.

At the end of the second half-line, however, there are many nouns that were feminine and also a number of masculine nouns that had a vowel in the nominative singular; for example: *hert* (OE *heorte*, f.), *blysse* (OE *bliss*, f.), *pryde* (OE *pryde*, f.), *synne* (OE *synn*, f.), *wille* (OE *willa*, m.), *lencþe* (OE *lengþu*, f.), *trawþe* (OE *treowþ*, f.), and *ende* (OE *ende*, m.).

Any explanation for these remarkable facts must address both metrical structure and historical phonology, for these are the two variables. The rules for syllable structure in (7) below are backward-looking, as are the rules for stress, and as indeed are some of the most salient literary qualities of the Alliterative Revival (the last two topics being the focus of several studies in progress but beyond the scope of this essay).

By my present understanding of the metrical paradigm, the general phonology of final -*e*, and the individual development of a few specific words, there are about two dozen lines ending with a native word that are not accounted for. As we find out more about the interacting factors, there are probably some lines that should be added to this list of 27 and some in the list that should be taken out. The scribal -*e* that appears on some of the words is not justified by my present formulation of principles: the nouns *Cam* (299), *day* (494), *toune* (721), *lawe* (OE *hlæw*, 992), *ly3t* (1272), *wowe* (1531), *felde* (1750), and *Gode* (1730, the only exception among 99 occurrences of *God* in the *Gawain*-poet); the adjectives *blake* (747), *best* (913), *olde* (1123), and *wode* (1558); the imperative *bete* (627, where an inorganic final -*e* is common in Chaucer); the auxiliary *schal* (1571, which Israel Gollancz emends by adding *be* at the end); and a dozen lines with adverbs, many of which are uncertain because of the possibility of analogical -*e* or the variable stress on phrasal adverbs: *nere* (414, 1585), þurȝout (1559), *aywhere* (1398, 1608), *þervpone* (1665), *away* (1241), *among* (1414), *þerof* (1499, 1507), *þerwyth* (1406, 1501).

Whether emendation is called for in 1571 or in any of the other verses is not the point of the present discussion, although the facts of this discussion might eventually lead to a consideration of certain principles of textual editing. In 1920 Robert J. Menner dismissed similar facts that had been noticed in 1908 by Julius Thomas: certain lines, said Menner, "where Thomas is obliged to resort to unlikely emendations, show that the weak ending cannot be accepted as a rule without exception."[9] The point for Menner was whether to emend specific lines in his edition. Although he made use of metrics, his aim was not the metrist's aim, and his questions and his emphasis were naturally different. The fact that a structure "cannot be accepted as a rule without exception" might settle one question for the editor (whether to emend on the basis of meter), but it raises a host of new questions for the metrist. To understand the meter one must ask why the structure occurs overwhelmingly as it does—in 92 percent of the lines according to Menner, or in 98 percent by my own count.

The argument of the essay to this point has been that final *-e* was essential in fourteenth-century alliterative meter because the end of the first half-line allowed an unstressed syllable optionally, but the end of the second half-line had an unstressed syllable 98 percent of the time. Rule-minded people can say that the end of the second half-line required an unstressed syllable; a few exceptions must then be acknowledged. People who are not rule-minded, such as Menner, can say, as he does, that there was a very strong tendency. I find it not very useful to talk about "tendencies," because tendencies are the result of interacting principles and not the principles themselves. A statement of tendencies is only a description of epiphenomena and not a very adequate one.

PHONOLOGICAL RULES

In the sporadic activity of scanning thousands of these lines during the past decade, I had generally found myself in agreement with metrists who concluded that the form of the verse is too uncertain to allow much beyond stating general tendencies, with alternative possibilities for any given line. It was only within the past three years that I discovered patterns I had missed for years. The evidence I have presented in this essay for the principles stated below is an exercise in mainstream historical metrics. We begin with patterns of occurrence and non-occurrence and keep the usual questions in mind: "What structures do not occur that should occur? Are there structures missing that would be expected on normal phonological and syntactic grounds? Can consistent principles be formulated to explain these present and missing patterns? Can the principles be called 'metrical'? Do the 'metrical' principles contradict either themselves or independent evidence such as that provided by historical phonology?"

What follows is a full list of rules to the extent that I presently understand them on the basis of the methods described above. Modifications and additions, based on additional evidence from the same principles, will be necessary, but the overall shape of the rules will hold. Some of the rules are similar to descriptions in traditional grammars. Some have not been stated in exactly this form before. Some flatly contradict the most familiar grammars, but only because the grammars do not take into account different registers.

In general, these rules require final -*e* in more structures than most current authorities recognize. This apparent expansion of the line by my reading is checked by a new formulation of the meter, which conversely limits the number of unstressed syllables in certain contexts.[10] Thus, there is a tension between the new phonological rules (which expand the line) and the new metrical rules (which constrain it), and there is the possibility for one set to contradict the other. To the extent that contradictions are avoided we have evidence in support of both sets of rules.

(6)   Phonology of final -*e*

Nouns

  1. Nouns from OE and ON that ended in a vowel in the
     nominative singular and nouns from OF that ended in a vowel

in the accusative singular have final -*e* in non-genitive singular
usage (e.g., *wy3e* < OE *wiga*; *kyrke* < ON *kirkja*; *prynce* <
OF *prince*).

2. Nouns from OE feminine declensions have a final -*e* in
   non-genitive singular usage (e.g., *þat styred synne* < OE
   synn, f., acc. sg. *synne*).

Adjectives

3. Adjectives from OE, ON, and OF that ended in a vowel in the
   uninflected form retain the vowel as -*e* (e.g., *clene* < OE
   clæne; *large* < OF *large*).

4. Monosyllabic adjectives from OE, ON, and OF have final -*e* in
   traditional weak contexts and in the plural:
   þe dérk dédé séé (*Cleanness* 1020; *derk* < OE *deorce*; *dede* <
   OE *deade*)

Verbs

5. Verbs from OE, ON, and OF have final -*e* in the infinitive.
6. Verbs from OE with preterites ending in -*ede*, -*edon*, and -*odon*
   have -*ede*. Verbs from OE with preterites ending in -*de* have
   -*de*. Verbs from OE with preterites ending in -*ode* (i.e., second
   class weak verbs in the preterite singular) have -*ed*.
7. Verbs from ON and OF form their preterites with -*ed* (without
   final -*e*).

Adverbs

8. Adverbs from OE with final -*e* retain the -*e*.
9. All adverbs ending in -*ly* retain the disyllabic structure of the
   two sources of that ending (OE -*lice* and ON -*liga*). Where the
   fricative is lost, the ending is assumed to be [lɪə].

Exceptions

10. The following words diverge in their individual developments
    from the general principles stated above:

    (a) Petrified datives: *on lyue*, *to grounde*, *to deþe*, *on fete*, *on
    horse*, *of (in) gold*.[11]

    (b) Disyllabic words from monosyllabic sources: *soþe* < OE
    soþ; *burne* < OE *beorn*; *schryfte* < OE *scrift*; *hy3t*, preterite
    sg., < OE *het*; *uche* < OE *ælc*; *there* < OE *þer*; *here* < OE
    her; *ofte* < OE *oft*; *lyte* < OE *lyt*.

    (c) Monosyllabic words from disyllabic sources: *bot* < OE
    butan, *hir* (except before a pl. noun) < OE *hire*; *þan*, conj., <
    OE *þanne* (but *þan*, adv., is disyllabic).

(d) Disyllabic words from trisyllabic sources: *apel* < OE
æpele; *mony* before a pl. noun < OE *monige* (but trisyllabic
monye < OE *monig* immediately before a sg. noun); *better* <
OE *betera*; *herk(k)en* < OE *heorcnian*; *rekken* < OE *recenian*
(a four-syllable source).

Metrical distribution suggests that the curious development of
meny(e) in (6.10d) resulted from the perception of the plural
ending -*e* as the definite article *a*—thus, the source of Middle and
Modern English "many a man" and the reversal of singular and
plural inflections in Middle English. *Uche* seems to have acquired
an -*e* by a similar process; it sometimes occurs as *uch a*, which I
take as metrically equivalent to the single word.

In all of my scansions, the various forms of "covered -*e*" are
expanded to give more syllables than the spelling might indicate.
Wern and *arn* are read as disyllabic when they are main verbs
(but monosyllabic when they are auxiliaries). *Lorde* is read as
disyllabic, as it was in Old English and in Middle English into
the fourteenth century. The only word that I read with a variable number of syllables, depending on the meter of the verse,
is *togeder*, which has both trisyllabic and quadrisyllabic forms in
Old English: *to-gædre*, *to-gædere*. Disallowing variable readings
is crucial to the argument supporting the rules in (6), because the
evidence rests on the idea that one part of the line requires no
more than one unstressed syllable, another part requires exactly
one unstressed syllable, and other parts require two or more unstressed syllables. It may be that various processes of elision operated in performance, but the advantages of disallowing elision in
the formulation of a theory should be clear. If a perspicuous paradigm emerges even without the flexibility of elision, then one has
a stronger theory because the data have been manipulated less.
The syllables of the line have been less shaped to conform to the
hypothesis.

Why should the reflexes of inflectional phonology in these texts
be so conservative, reflecting features of Old English? The historical grammars of Middle English state that final -*e* had disappeared from the spoken language of the North and Northwest
Midlands at this time (although it must be remembered that the

statements of the historical grammars were based on the same kind of evidence that we are examining here, and in many instances the evidence was less fully analyzed). To say that final *-e* was preserved in poetic texts is not, of course, to say that it was preserved in every instance in the spoken language. The spread of a sound change is a complex matter with conservative and innovative usages coexisting for a period. In other respects as well the texts of the Alliterative Revival are backward-looking, and if older forms were available, it is not surprising that the poets would have used them.

THE STRUCTURE OF THE EVIDENCE AND THE ARGUMENT

Whatever the cultural and literary reasons for retention of final *-e*, however, it is important to emphasize that I arrived at the rules regulating its status from purely internal metrical and linguistic structures. For reasons that I do not fully understand, the process of extracting hypotheses from a limited corpus and then testing the hypotheses against an expanded corpus of similar texts strikes some observers as circular.[12]

Therefore, it is worth recapitulating the structure of the evidence and the argument. The original frame within which I hypothesized the rules in (6) was the final syllable at the end of each hemistich. The consistent patterns that began to materialize in this slot, during the course of scanning thousands of verses, led to conclusions about the other slots in the hemistich. The end of each half-line, in effect, cast a network of implicature leftwards. We can sketch the frame for the final syllable as follows:

(7)

First half-line	Second half-line
_____ (x) (x)	_____ x

The parentheses around the two x's of the first half-line indicate that there can be one, or two, or no unstressed syllables in that position. The single x without parentheses in the second half-line indicates that there must be exactly one unstressed syllable at the end of the long line.

Let us posit the pattern in (7): the first half-line can end with no unstressed syllable, or with one or two unstressed syllables; the second half-line must end with exactly one unstressed syllable. If we examine the poems and find at the end of the first half-line words such as *men*, *halden*, and *parlement* (with, respectively, no unstressed syllable, one unstressed syllable, and two unstressed syllables), then we have evidence for the proposed first-half pattern. If, further, we find at the end of the second half-line words such as *halden*, with one unstressed syllable, but no words such as *men* and also no words such as *parlement*, then we have evidence for the proposed pattern for the second half-line. The present essay has followed exactly this method, grouping the various classes of words according to their origins.

As for *-e*, if the phonological rules specify no final unstressed syllable for a certain class of lexical items, and those items show up at the end of the second half-line, then we have evidence against either the phonological rules, the metrical pattern, or both. If it happens, for example, that Old Norse nouns with monosyllabic stems show up at the end of the second half-line, then we have to conclude that there is an error somewhere in our dual hypothesis. As we have seen, such nouns are carefully avoided in the final position of the fourteenth-century alliterative line. To come back to the beginning, then, the question to ask is "Why?" Any adequate theory of Middle English alliterative meter must answer this question. The choice between competing theories depends upon the generality and economy of the answer.

The direction of the present theory accords with observations that A. T. E. Matonis has succinctly made: "The poets as a rule prefer a syllabically longer a-line; they allow a larger number of syllables in anacrusis in the a-line; many more a-lines end in double feminine endings; the a-line more frequently supports extended verses; and the a-lines are characteristically heavier in narrative value." [13] The patterns for final *-e* outlined above both confirm these observations and make them more definite.

They can be made more definite still. The phonological rules in (6) are open to revision and supplementation, and the lines along which these adjustments can be made should be clear. The changes will involve details in the rules and statements about the development of individual words that are exceptions. For example, at one time I hypothesized that dative -*e* was productive in these texts, and I scanned all lines accordingly. On noticing that most of what I took to be dative -*e* occurred in feminine nouns, I changed the hypothesis to eliminate dative -*e* and posited instead a final -*e* on all nouns that were feminine in Old English. I then went back, as is necessary whenever assumptions are revised, and changed all the scansions of my working corpus to accord with the new hypothesis, which indeed accounts much more adequately for the facts. However, I would be surprised if *all* feminine nouns from Old English acquired a final -*e*. As the diagnostic contexts identify those nouns that did not (so far I have not identified any), further revisions in the rules, or additions to the specified exceptions will have to be made.

More important than the specific rules of this essay, then, is the outline of a self-confirming method that will apply to some sixty thousand lines of fourteenth-century Middle English. The process is time-consuming because of the need to revise earlier scansions as hypotheses are revised. However, the structure of the argument makes explicit the kind of empirical evidence that can be brought in support or refutation of the hypotheses. It establishes a firm piece of ground for studying the phonology of final -*e* and the meter of these West Midlands texts.

NOTES

1. "Langland's Dialect," *Medium Ævum* 54 (1985):243. See also "Chaucerian Final '-e,' " *Notes and Queries* 217 (1972):445–48.

2. See, for example, Karl Luick, *Historische Grammatik der englishchen Sprache, I* (Leipzig: Tauchnitz, 1921), Section 473; see also Richard Jordan, *Handbook of Middle English Grammar: Phonology*, trans. and rev. Eugene J. Crook (The Hague: Mouton, 1974), §§138–41.

3. Marie Borroff, *Sir Gawain and the Green Knight: A Stylistic and Metrical Study* (New Haven: Yale University Press, 1962).

4. Angus McIntosh, "Early Middle English Alliterative Verse," in *Middle English Alliterative Poetry*, ed. David Lawton (Cambridge, Eng.: Brewer, 1982), 20–33.

5. John H. Fisher, "Chancery and the Emergence of Standard Written English in the Fifteenth Century," *Speculum* 52 (1977):891.

6. Lines cited are from the edition by J. J. Anderson, *Cleanness* (Manchester, Eng.: Manchester University Press, 1977).

7. Charles Sanders Peirce, *The Philosophy of Peirce: Selected Writings*, ed. Justus Buchler (London: Routledge and Kegan Paul, 1940), p. 151.

8. Two of these are the word *(h)ayre* (OF *(h)eir*), which was clearly disyllabic in Early Middle English and into the fourteenth century (see the citations in the *MED*). The others are *vale* (673), *dyspyt* (821), *rounde* (1121), *pere* (1336), *palle* (1384), *clere* (1456), and *state* (1708).

9. Robert J. Menner, ed., *Purity: A Middle English Poem* (New Haven: Yale University Press, 1920), lvni.

10. See my "Middle English Meter and Its Theoretical Implications," *Yearbook of Langland Studies* 2 (1988):47–69.

11. In *Chaucer's Irregular -E* (New York: King's Crown, 1942), Ruth B. McJimsey treats the first five of these phrases as petrified datives in Chaucer and *of golde* as uncertain.

12. This comment has been a recurring theme in the productive exchanges that I have had with Hoyt Duggan, including a debate at the Twenty-second International Congress on Medieval Studies at Western Michigan University. The presentations were titled, "What Constitutes Evidence? An Empiricist's Approach to Middle English Grammar and Meter" (Duggan) and "What Constitutes Evidence? A Rationalist's Approach to Middle English Grammar and Meter" (Cable).

13. A. T. E. Matonis, "A Reexamination of the Middle English Alliterative Long Line," *Modern Philology* 81 (1984):346.

Standardising Shakespeare's Non-Standard Language

N. F. Blake

As the English language became more regulated in spelling and vocabulary through the efforts of teachers and the availability of dictionaries and grammars, it became possible for writers to exploit the differences which were seen to exist between this standardised version of the language and other varieties. It is characteristic of these other varieties that they have no standardised form, for to some extent they are characterised by speakers of the standard language by their difference from the standard rather than by any internal consistency. As such varieties sank lower in esteem, it was not considered worthwhile to devote time to standardising them because the aim of education was to eradicate their use, not to perpetuate them by providing them with some spurious respectability through regularising their spelling.

As these varieties became associated with provincial and uneducated speakers, however, they were picked up by writers of literary works to provide some colour and verisimilitude to their portrayal of character. But these writers never attempted to provide a complete representation of the speech of such people, for it was usually sufficient if readers understood that a different, i.e., less prestigious, variety of language was being indicated. It was sufficient that certain features should be introduced, and even these were not found at all regularly.[1] This practice naturally opened the possibility that scribes or printers who were issuing the text at a later date could tamper with this linguistic representation to provide a more coherent and consistent representation of this non-standard variety. Changes of this nature were made because as the use of non-standard language grew in literary works, it became increasingly standardised so that readers would have little difficulty in understanding that the speaker was indeed non-standard. This situation raises two interesting and related editorial problems: determining what the author originally wrote in his representation of non-standard language and how far in modern editions we should reproduce what he wrote or accept what has become convention through the process of standardisation carried out in subsequent editions.

Before turning to Shakespeare I should like to illustrate some of these points from *The Canterbury Tales*, one of the earliest literary texts which attempts to exploit the difference between standard and non-standard varieties. In the Reeve's Tale there are two undergraduates from Cambridge who are said to come from far in the North. Chaucer gives them a variety of language which has northern features in it, and we are clearly supposed to see this difference as significant. Chaucer portrays the northern dialect through lexis, syntax, and orthography. A number of words, mainly of Scandinavian origin, are found in the speech of the undergraduates, though many of them are occasionally found elsewhere in the writings of Chaucer and his contemporaries. Most lexical features are not unambiguously northern. Standardisation had not proceeded far enough at this stage for that to be true. The bulk of the northern characterisation is carried through the spelling system indicating phonological and morphological differences. Words which are normally spelt with *o* or *oo* in Chaucer's English appear with *a* in the undergraduates' language: *banes* (for *bones*) and *ra* (for *ro* "roedeer"). Similarly Chaucer's normal group *-lc* appears as *-lk* in words like *whilk* (for *whilc* "which") and *swilk* (for *swilc* "such"). Morphological features include the use of *-(e)s* for *-(e)th* as the ending of the third-person singular of the present tense, and the omission of initial *y-* and the inclusion of final *-n* in past participial forms: *falles* (for *falleth*) and *lorn* (for *ylore*). Syntactical changes include northern forms of the present tense of the verb "to be" such as *I is*, *thow is*, and *they ar* (for *I am*, *thou art*, and *they ben*).

These northern forms are introduced only sporadically in the Hengwrt manuscript, which is now considered to be the oldest and

most authoritative manuscript of the poem. Later scribes reacted
in two quite opposite ways. Some northern forms were replaced
by southern ones: the word *il* is frequently replaced by *euel*.
But many northern forms which are not in Hengwrt have been introduced in later manuscripts. New *a* forms appear, such as *swa*
(for *so*) and *tald* (for *told*). Additional past participles are give
a final *-n*, as in *stoln* (for *stole*). More interestingly, new forms
altogether appear. The southern *behoues*, *take*, and *if* can appear
in the northern forms *boes*, *taa*, and *gif*. Initial *wh-* is replaced
by *qw-* in some manuscripts, and the *i* of *is* appears as *e* to give
es. The phrase *get vs som* is changed into *gar vs haue*. It would
appear as though scribes were familiar with the northern dialect
and wished to introduce its features into the speech of the northern undergraduates even where Chaucer had not done so. They
realised what Chaucer was up to and wanted to make sure that his
point came across to the readers. Some scribes were clearly trying
to out-Chaucer Chaucer.[2]

When we consider Shakespeare the same principles may apply,
but there are other problems. Although the First Folio of 1623
represents the primary source for the text of most Shakespearian
plays, many of them were issued earlier in individual quartos.
Some plays appeared in several quartos. It is not clear always what
the relationship between quarto(s) and Folio is. Some quartos may
be memorial reconstructions and others may be official texts. The
Folio may be based on the quarto either in part or in full. The
Folio text may represent a Shakespearian revision. I would suggest
that this uncertainty is not material to the general discussion since
the quarto text or texts represent an earlier stage or stages in the
text's transmission, no matter precisely how one stage relates to
the other. When it comes to representing non-standard language
it may not matter precisely if one text did not use the previous
edition as copytext, for whoever prepared the new edition had to
respond to this type of language and to take a view as to what
the author intended and how an audience might be made aware
of those intentions. He had to take a position as to what features
should be there. Because we are dealing with printed books it will
not usually be possible to tell whether changes were introduced

by an editor or a compositor. As the First Folio was set up by several compositors, we may well find that different approaches to standardisation are exemplified in different plays. All we can hope to do in a short essay like this is to note certain trends.

It may help to focus on some of these questions if a short passage from one of the plays is considered in depth. In *King Lear* Edgar leads his father, Gloucester, towards Dover where Gloucester throws himself off the cliff, or so the old man thinks. There they encounter Oswald, the steward, who tries to kill Gloucester to curry favour with his masters. In this encounter Edgar adopts a different speech mode, which is that used in contemporary plays for the peasant class in the south of England. There are three short speeches in this assumed dialect (IV, vi, 232-42), numbered one to three below. I give these three speeches as they occur in the "1608" Quarto, the First Folio, and a modern edition, the Arden text edited by Kenneth Muir.[3]

"1608" Quarto
1. Chill not let goe without cagion.
2. Good Gentleman goe your gate, let poore voke passe, and chud haue beene swaggar'd out of my life, it would not haue beene so long by a vortnight, nay come not neare the old man, keepe out cheuore ye, or ile trie whether your costerd or my bat be the harder, ile be plaine with you.
3. Chill pick your teeth sir, come, no matter for your foyns.

First Folio
1. Chill not let go Zir,
   Without vurther 'casion.
2. Good gentleman goe your gate, and let poore volke passe: and 'chud ha' bin zwaggerd out of my life, 'twould not ha' bin zo long as 'tis, by a vortnight. Nay, come not neere th'old man: keepe out che vor'ye, or ice try whither your Costard, or my Ballow be the harder; chill be plaine with you.
3. Chill picke your teeth Zir: come, no matter vor your foynes.

Arden Edition
1. Chill not let go, sir, without vurther 'casion.
2. Good gentleman, go your gait, and let poor volk pass. And 'chud ha' bin zwagger'd out of my life, 'twould not ha' bin zo long as 'tis

by a vortnight. Nay, come not near th'old man; keep out, che vor'
ye, or ise try whither your costard or my ballow be the harder. Chill
be plain with you.

3. Chill pick your teeth, zir. Come; no matter vor your foins.

I have put "1608" in quotation marks because, although the
first quarto was originally printed at that time, the edition was
corrected as it went through the press and subsequently reprinted
in 1619, although the date of printing is still given as 1608. The
most corrected copy of the quarto has at least 150 corrections
introduced into it, including two in passage 2. What is given as
costerd and *bat* above appeared in the earlier printings as *coster*
and *battero*. There is also a correction in passage 3, for the first
word *Chill* had appeared in the first quarto as *Ile*. From these
corrections it appears as though there was a process of standardisation, which was continued in the Folio text. There is no reason
to believe that these corrections were made by Shakespeare, but
equally there is little likelihood that the spellings in the first quarto
reflect precisely what Shakespeare wrote.

Let us now look at these versions in greater detail.[4] The use of
Ile as an abbreviated form of *I will* is not regarded as characteristic
of a peasant dialect speaker and so this form is gradually removed
from his language. We have just seen that the first quarto had
Ile in the third passage, which was corrected in the later quarto
printings to *Chill*. It may be because passage 3 stands by itself
and *Ile* is its first word, and hence very noticeable, that the word
was changed to *Chill*. This brings passage 3 into line with passage 1. It is characteristic that words which stand out, and this
applies particularly to those which begin speeches or sentences,
are liable to standardisation. Once this word appeared as *Chill* it
remained with that form. However, there are two examples of *ile*
in passage 2. The second of these, which comes right at the end
of the passage, is not corrected in the quarto texts. In the Folio it
appears as *Chill*. As it stands at the head of what is virtually a new
sentence, for it follows a semicolon in the Folio and a full stop
in the Arden edition, it is not surprising that it should have been
emended to *Chill*. It has kept this form in modern editions. The
other example of *ile* occurs within a sentence and seems to have

attracted less attention to itself. In the Folio this *ile* is corrected to *ice*, and in modern editions this appears as *ise* or *ice*, though sometimes with an initial capital letter as *Ise* or *Ice*. Those that keep the actual spelling *ice* assume that the *c* represents [s].

This change of *ile* to *ice* is of some interest. One might have expected a standardiser to introduce *chill* rather than *ice* for *ile*, since *chill* is clearly the form which is otherwise characteristic of this dialect in the play and which was substituted for *ile* elsewhere. It seems improbable that a man who was correcting *ile* to *chill* in one sentence would correct it to *ice* in another. This raises the possibility that *ice* is from a different version which perhaps has authorial authority. But this raises the same problem in a slightly different form: did Shakespeare want to represent this dialect as having *chill* or as having *ice* as the contracted form of *I will*? It is true that writers may introduce more than one variant of a form in their representation of non-standard language, though this is less likely to happen in such a short passage. The other possibility is that the Folio's *ice* is a misprint. This could be explained on the basis that the compositor misread the *l* of *ile* as a long *s* and then represented the *s* as a *c*, which in this environment is perfectly possible, as in modern *mice*. The form *ice/ise* is perfectly acceptable as a dialect form. Although some have considered it as a northern dialect form, it does occur in modern southwestern dialects and equivalent forms, such as *Ise*, *thouse*, and *wese*, are recorded in *Gammer Gurton's Needle* (III, iii, 42, 44, 47).[5] The fact that it is a possible form is not the same as saying that it was intended by Shakespeare, who appears to have used the *chill* form alone. It may well be that modern editions should revert to *ile* or emend to *chill*. The former would represent the standard colloquial contraction and thus illustrate the influence of the standard on the dialect; the latter would be the form that was standard in stage versions of the southern dialect.

It is also clear from the Folio text that its editor or compositor realised that Shakespeare was representing the southern dialect through the voicing of initial *f* and *s* to *v* and *z*. But the voiced forms are not introduced as fully in the quarto as in the Folio. The quarto has two examples of initial *v*- for *f*- in *voke* and *vortnight*.

The Folio has introduced a further change to *v-* in *vor* in passage 3. This last case is a preposition, whereas the other two forms are nouns and so carry stress. It may well be that the original version insisted on this change only with lexical words like nouns. Neither quarto nor Folio introduces an initial *v-* in *foyns*, even though it is a noun. The reason for this may be the relative rarity of the word. It is a loan from French and occurs a few times elsewhere in Shakespeare as a verb "to make a thrust in fencing." This is the only time it is used as a noun. If as a noun it had appeared with initial *v-*, it might be difficult for readers and listeners to recognise what it meant. One should perhaps add that *foyns* is not a word likely to have been part of a peasant's vocabulary. It should be noticed that the Folio introduces the word *vurther* in passage 1, which had not occurred in the quarto text, and this word is given the dialect initial *v-*. More changes occur in the case of initial *s-/z-*. In the quarto text there are no examples of this voicing at all. Three words could have been given the *z-* form, and they are *swaggar'd*, *so*, and *sir*. All are given *z-* forms in the Folio, and an additional example of *Zir* is included by the Folio in passage 1. In other words the Folio editor accepted that the voicing of *s-* occurs in the same dialects as that of *f-*, and so existing words and new words beginning with that sound were changed accordingly. What had been a suggestion of the southern dialect in the quarto has become much more consistent and clear in the Folio.

The next difference I wish to focus on between the texts is more a part of representing colloquial language than an example of dialect. It revolves around the use of the apostrophe.[6] In the quarto text the apostrophe is used sparingly and indicates the omission of a letter, usually within a word as in *swaggar'd*. In the Folio it occurs more frequently. It still represents the omission of a letter or letters, though in these passages the omission occurs at beginning or end of the word rather than internally. The form *swaggar'd* of the quarto appears as *zwaggerd* in the Folio, where the absence of the apostrophe might indeed be intended to suggest a non-standard form since the occurrence of an apostrophe in standardised English was common enough in this position. Modern editions replace the apostrophe here. The forms *chill* and *chud*, which are the dialect representations of *I will* (or *I'll*) and *I would* (or *I'd*) have no apostrophes in the quarto, though they are based on the variant form of *I* which is *ich*. In one instance in the Folio *chud* is given an apostrophe at the beginning to give *'chud*, as though to indicate that the dialect form is an abbreviated version of *ichud*.

The effect of this apostrophe is to downgrade the form even further, for it suggests that not only is the form dialectal, but this particular example of it is a sloppy pronunciation in which the initial *i* is omitted. Modern editors have been uncertain what to do about this apostrophe: some, like Muir, keep it, but others leave it out. Those that keep it do not usually introduce it into the other forms like *chill* or *che vor'ye* where it would be just as appropriate if the punctuation is to be standardised. The apostrophe is also used in the Folio reading *'casion*, where the quarto has *cagion*. The change of the form of the word and the introduction of the apostrophe make the form simply a clipped pronunciation of the standard word, for *'casion* must be understood as an aphetic form of *occasion*. It is not dialectal any more; it is simply colloquial. But we will return to this word shortly. Two examples of *haue* in the quarto appear as *ha'* in the Folio, presumably because the form *ha'*, which is not specifically dialectal, was considered appropriate for a speaker of low-class origins. Similarly *it would* is reduced to *'twould* in the Folio, and in an additional phrase the form *'tis* occurs rather than *it is*. What had been *the old man* in the quarto appears as *th'old man* in the Folio, and the reason for this change must be the same. In all these cases modern editors follow the Folio, presumably because they agree with its compositor that the abbreviated forms are more colloquial and so more likely to be found in a dialect speaker.

This does run the risk of confusing colloquial speech with dialect speech. One final use of the apostrophe is particularly interesting. What had appeared in the quarto texts as *cheuore ye* is represented in the Folio as *che vor'ye*. Modern linguists are uncertain what the etymology of this phrase is, though *che* and *ye* are the first and second personal pronouns respectively. The *uore/vor* may be a variant of *warn* or *warrant*, though Kökeritz is quite adamant that the latter is the correct interpretation.[7] Alexander Gill has the form *chi vör yi* in 1621. If *uore/vor* is a form of *warrant*, the interesting question is whether this was known to the Folio compositor or even to Shakespeare. Was the apostrophe added to indicate this, or was it added simply because the compositor did not know what the word was but thought an apostrophe would add the appropriate impression of colloquial or dialectal speech? The latter seems the more probable. Modern editors are uncertain what to do with it: some keep it and others leave it out.

Some spellings are changed from quarto to Folio. Many of these, such as the inclusion or omission of final -*e*, are arbitrary and may at best reflect compositorial prejudices. Some may be more important. The quarto has the spelling *voke* which later versions emend to *volke*. The *l* in this consonantal group had almost certainly fallen by this time and so the two spellings do not indicate variant pronunciations. But the spelling with the *l* was now regular in print, and it may have been included in later quartos and the Folio because it was not part of normal dialect representation. Its omission in the first quarto may have been meant to indicate dialect. Modern editors normally have the spelling with *l*.

The past participle *beene* in the quarto appears as *bin* in the Folio and most modern editions keep this spelling, although in the rest of the play *been* is the common spelling. There is evidence that in the London of Shakespeare's day *been* could be pronounced with long or short *i*. But in this context the link of *bin* with the shortened form *ha'* suggests strongly that there was an attempt to suggest colloquial or substandard pronunciation. The form *been* was restored in the Fourth Folio. The spelling *ar* in *swaggar'd* is probably not significant as it occurs in a weakly stressed syllable, but the variation of *er* and *ar* was sometimes used by Shakespeare to suggest dialect or colloquial pronunciation. If the spelling was suggestively used, the point was lost on later editors who all have *er* here. In passage 2, the quarto has *whether*, which appears in the Folio as *whither*, and this form is kept by some modern editors like Muir. Some words with short *e* do appear with *i* in Shakespeare and other writers of the time. Today the form is considered somewhat substandard, though that may not have been the case then. Its introduction in this scene is almost certainly supposed to indicate low-class pronunciation. In modern times we accept this *i* form in some words like *divil* "devil," but it is not regarded as a regular sign of non-standard language. Probably many modern editors do not keep the *i* spelling because they are worried that readers will confuse the spelling *whither* "whether" with the word *whither* "to where." The quarto reading of *costerd* I have given is a corrected form, for the earliest version had *coster*. So there is a change in this form from *coster* through *costerd* to *costard*. The absence of final *d* after liquids and nasals was quite common in the sixteenth century and is a marker of colloquial speech rather than of dialect pronunciation. Since the word itself is colloquial, it may well have been felt that further indications of its status like the fall of final -*d* were unnecessary. The change from *er* to *ar* is the reverse of what happened in *swaggar'd*. But as *ar* is the spelling found elsewhere in this word in Shakespeare, it may have been accepted that was its proper form. If the spelling *coster* was intended to accentuate the low status of this word, the point was soon lost as editors standardised it.

The word *cagion* we have already mentioned. It is normally assumed to be a variant of *casion*, an aphetic form of *occasion*. The derivation is far from certain, and if true would perhaps indicate that *cagion* had more or less adopted the identity of a separate word. It seems not to have been understood by later editors, for it was replaced by *vurther 'casion*. Unless one understands the quarto word to be a misprint, even though it survives in all editions of the quarto text, it is surprising that it is not found in modern editions, for it is unlikely that a compiler or actor working from memorial reconstruction would insert such an unusual form unless it had some textual standing. One other word needs comment. The original quarto text had *battero*, which was corrected in later quartos to *bat* and replaced altogether by the Folio with *ballow*. Modern editors keep *ballow*, though it is not certain whether it has any authority. It may be that *battero* is an attempt to represent *ballow*, but it is surely more likely that *ballow*, which is a dialect word, was introduced as an emendation into the text. *Battero* is an unknown word and is less likely to have been introduced in a memorial reconstruction. If it is original, it would imply an instrument for battering, which would be comic rather than dialect. It could even be intended as a substandard variation of *battery*. The form *bat* is surely a simplification of *battero*, because that word was not understood.

As for syntax the only point which may need comment is the addition of *and* in passage 2 by the Folio, an addition which is repeated in modern editions. It is characteristic of some representations of non-standard language that they present a jerky style through the omission of conjunctions or other grammatical words. This may have been intended here, but if so, the intention has become lost. The whole of passage 2 does proceed in short, somewhat awkward clauses, and this sense of incomplete command of the language is increased if the *and* is left out.

If one takes the passage as a whole one can certainly detect certain tendencies. The vocabulary is generally not touched, but unusual words or forms are made more recognisable by altering the words or their spellings. The chances of a completely strange word like *cagion* or *battero* surviving are slim; this is after all dialect speech rather than comedy. Syntactic features, if intended, are also likely to be ironed out. On the other hand, certain features are likely to be included or to be made more regular, such as spellings which indicate dialect or colloquial pronunciation. Forms or expressions recognised as dialect are extended, like *chill*, and spellings which indicate a provincial pronunciation, such as voicing of initial *f* and *s*, are made more regular. More interestingly, some spellings which can only be considered colloquial, such as *ha'* for *haue* and *bin* for *beene*, are introduced. But these forms are stock features readily found in other Shakespearian passages. It should be emphasised that these changes only scratch the surface, for there is no attempt to introduce further spelling changes. There is no attempt to alter the spelling of words like *-night*, for example. Only those spellings which had become traditional in representation of dialect or colloquial speech are introduced. The effect, therefore, is to make the language standardised: it has lost some of its unusual features and it has become more regular in its deviation.

It is time now to look at one or two other plays to see whether they reflect the same changes. First I will consider Act II, scene i, of *King Henry IV, Part I*, for although the characters there are not necessarily dialect speakers, it is often assumed that their language is substandard. I shall not reproduce the text in detail as I shall consider only certain features of this scene. This play was printed in quarto before its appearance in the First Folio, and the quarto text went through several revisions. It is an interesting reversal of modern editorial attitudes that, whereas in *King Lear* editors tend to follow the language of the Folio, in *King Henry IV, Part I* they tend to follow that of the quarto. Their preference for the quarto text in this case is precisely because editors feel the Folio text has gone through a process of standardisation which robs the play of some of its character. It is a feature of this scene that several sentences exhibit omission of article, pronoun, or conjunction. As early as the Cambridge edition of 1864 this type of omission was recognised as an indicator of what is frequently referred to as "rusticity," [8] and this has no doubt influenced all subsequent editors. The following examples occur. The quarto text is quoted with the Folio addition included at the appropriate place in square brackets.

1. [the] poore iade is wroong in the withers.
2. since Robin [the] Ostler died.
3. and twere not as good [a] deede as drinke to break the pate on thee.
4. or rather not [to] pray to her.
5. you are more beholding to the night then to [the] Ferneseed

One or two of these changes are introduced in later quartos, though the greatest change comes in the Folio. However, one or two examples are not changed even in the Folio so that *Poore fellow neuer ioied since the prise of Oates rose* has remained without an initial article.

There are some other changes in this scene. As is typical of the play as a whole, the oaths and asseverations which occur so frequently in the quarto are either omitted or replaced in the Folio. In this scene *by the Masse* and *Gods bodie* are omitted and *by God* is replaced by *I pray ye*. This change naturally reduces the colloquial nature of all the prose scenes in the play. There are a few spelling changes that reflect some of the changes made in *King Lear*. The past participle *bin* of the quarto twice becomes *beene* in the Folio. The word *prethe*, which has several forms in the quarto, is regularised to *prethee* even when the quarto has *pray thee*. And the word *lanterne* is spelt as *lanthorne* in the Folio. Apart from the first, these changes are probably not significant. The first suggests that the colloquial nature of this scene is not being kept by the compositor. This may also be suggested by the change of *be* to *is* in *I thinke this be the most villainous house* and by the change of *King christen* to *King in Christendome*. However, there are certain contrary indications. There is rather more elision represented through the use of the apostrophe in the Folio than in the earlier texts. *An it* in the opening speech becomes *an't*, and later in the scene *hee is* becomes *hee's*. And *he* is replaced by *a* in one line, which may be intended to suggest a proverbial or folksy saying. The quarto *lend me thy lantern (quoth he)* becomes the Folio *Lend mee thy Lanthorne (quoth-a)*. It is recognised by many editors that this last example is more colloquial and so some of them retain it in their text, although most modern ones remain faithful to the quarto.

The language of Act II, scene i, was not sufficiently different for it to have attracted the attention of the editor or compositor of the Folio. It is not in dialect and it has no unusual words, apart from the humorous ones used by Gadshill. It would not, therefore, be earmarked for special editorial attention. It was treated in much the same way as other prose passages. More elision may well have been introduced, but other features which may have been originally intended to produce a colloquial effect were incorporated by the compositors. The single example of *quoth-a* which was inserted in the text probably owes its presence more to the wish to create an archaism in the form of a pretended quotation than to an attempt to introduce a colloquialism as such.[9] No attempt is made to create a language which has more dialect or substandard forms.

When we come to *Henry V*, we encounter both dialect language —because the captains come from Wales, Scotland, and Ireland

—and colloquial speech among people like Pistol. This play was also published in quarto before appearing in the First Folio; again this quarto was reprinted and corrected. There are, however, more important problems with this quarto. It is now widely accepted that the quarto text is based on an actor's memorial reconstruction and that the Folio was printed from Shakespeare's manuscript. There are many omissions in the quarto as compared with the Folio, and some may be attributable as much to political expedience as to faulty memory. As far as this particular investigation is concerned, these omissions are particularly significant for the characters of Captain Macmorris, who speaks a form of Irish English, and Captain Jamy, a Scotsman. Neither appears in the quarto version at all. In other words the representation of dialect in the 1600 version appears only in the language of the Welshman Captain Fluellen. The only other captain to appear in this version is the Englishman Captain Gower, whose language is not deviant. Let us start therefore by considering Fluellen's language.

He appears first in Act III, scene ii, before Harfleur. His first words in the quarto are *Godes plud*, an oath which is omitted in the Folio and most modern editions.[10] The word *plud* introduces one aspect of Fluellen's language, namely his unvoicing of labial *b*, particularly when it occurs initially in words. The *u* may or may not be significant, but the representation of vowel sounds in the roman alphabet is far from reliable. It is used in the Folio to represent the Scots variety of *oo* by Captain Jamy, and so it seems unlikely this spelling would have survived into the Folio if the expression had been kept. One may assume it was dropped because the Folio frequently omits such oaths. *Gods plud* is found again at Act IV, scene i, in the quarto, but again it is omitted in the Folio. However, in Act IV, scene vii, the quarto's *Gode plut* appears in the Folio as '*Sblud*, which may indicate that the form *plud/plut* did appear in the Folio's copytext. In this instance *plut* has changed both initial *p-* to *b-* and final *-d* to *-t*. Fluellen then goes on: *vp to the breaches*. In the Folio *breaches* appears in the singular. It is a feature of his speech to use plurals where the singular is found in the standard, and we shall see that the Folio has many more examples than the quarto. However, the context here could admit of one or more breaches, and so it is uncertain which was intended.

The next speech of Fluellen in the quarto introduces several features which are worth looking at in some detail:

> Looke you, tell the Duke it is not so good
> To come to the mines: the concuaueties is otherwise.
> You may discusse to the Duke, the enemy is digd
> Himselfe fiue yardes vnder the countermines:
> By *Iesus* I thinke heele blowe vp all
> If there be no better direction.[11]

This passage is written as verse in the quarto, but as prose in the Folio. It is introduced by *Looke you*, which becomes one of the phrases associated with Fluellen. This phrase appears twice again in this speech as it occurs in the Folio. In the quarto *the mines* may or may not be an example of the Welsh use of a plural for a singular because either is appropriate here. In the Folio the plural for singular is made explicit since another sentence *the Mynes is not according to the disciplines of the Warre* is included. Indeed that sentence not only has plural *Mynes* with singular *is*, it also has plural *disciplines* where a singular might be expected. But the quarto does have the plural *concauities* (which is meant by *concuaueties*) with singular *is*. Instead of *enemy* in the quarto, the Folio has *athuersarie*, which is a more learned word and suggests Fluellen's reading of the books of war. Where the quarto reads *By Iesus I thinke heele blowe vp all*, the Folio has *by Cheshu, I thinke a will plowe vp all*. The text in the quarto is not of a dialect nature at all; it has at best the colloquial *heele* instead of *he will*. But the Folio introduces the spelling *Cheshu* for *Iesus*, and so gives a decidedly dialect feel to the word; it also alters *blowe* to *plowe* and thus carries further the introduction of unvoiced *p-* for labial *b-*. It replaces the quarto *he* with *a*, which as we have seen is a colloquial or substandard pronunciation—or rather a writing which was used to suggest that. This *a* can hardly be thought of as a dialect phenomenon; it is a feature that is often added to the language of non-standard speakers almost as a kind of reflex action. Finally we may note that the quarto's *direction* is turned into a plural in the Folio.

Some of these features can now be considered in the play as a whole. The change of initial *b-* to *p-* does not occur regularly in either version, but there are far more examples in the Folio than in the quartos. To some extent this may be because there is more speech allocated to Fluellen in the Folio, and passages which are in the Folio but not in the quartos are more likely than not to exhibit the change of *b-* to *p-*. These include *pridge* (twice), *praue*, (twice), *pashfull* (where the quarto has *queamish*), *petter*, and *peseech* (where the quarto has *desire*). The examples where both versions have no change at all include *bridge*. There are only a few occasions where the quarto has an initial *p-* where the Folio has *b-*; they include two examples of *plind* (Folio *blinde*), in addition to the examples of *plud*/*plut* which we have already commented on. There are some examples where both have the change of *b-* to *p-*; and these include *praue*, *plew* (for *blue*), and *plesse* (for *bless*). Most significant, though, are the large number of examples where the Folio has introduced an initial *p-* which was not found in the quarto. These include *pride* (twice), *pible bable* (for *bible bable*), *poyes* (for *boyes*), *porne* (for *born*, three times), *pig* (for *big*, three times), *praines* (for *braine*), *plood* (for *blood*), *peare* (for *beare*), *prawles and prabbles* (for *brawls and brabbles*), *prings* (for *brings*), *peate* (for *beate*), and *ploodie* (for *bloody*). The examples of *pig* occur in the phrase *Alexander the pig*, in which *big* is contrasted with *great*. The introduction of *p-* for *b-* in the Folio tends to detract from this contrast between *big* and *great*, which is clearer in the quarto. It would seem as though the Folio editor recognised this change as characteristic of Welsh speech and introduced it as frequently as he could. It is interesting in this connexion to notice that on one occasion in the Folio initial *d-* is replaced by initial *t-*, for where the quarto has *S. Dauies* the Folio has *S. Tauies*.

Another characteristic of Welsh speech was the phrase *look you*. This, however, is found rather more frequently in the quarto than the Folio, even though the amount of speech given to Fluellen in the Folio is much greater than that found in the quarto. In fact there are six examples found in the quarto which are not in the

Folio as against five in the Folio not found in the quarto. It suggests that the use of this phrase was rather indiscriminate. However, we should remember that in the quarto Fluellen's speech is given as a kind of verse, and this may have influenced the retention of the phrase in most instances. It should perhaps also be mentioned that in one case the quarto's *looke you* is changed by the Folio to *marke you*, and in another it becomes *I warrant you*. In the quarto there is an example of *like you now* which is not repeated in the Folio but which may represent a compositorial mistake for *loke you now*. We have already noted that the Folio tends to omit asseverations like *By Jesus*. Several examples of this phrase occur in the quarto text, and when they occur they always have the form *Iesus* or *Iesu*; they are never given a variant spelling. The form *Cheshu* is found in Fluellen's opening speeches in the Folio, but generally where the quarto has *Iesus* this is omitted or rewritten to something like *Ile assure you* in the Folio. In one instance only is the word kept and then it is written *Ieshu*, which is supposed to represent, presumably, a Welsh change of *s* to *sh*. This is the only word in which this change occurs, which is perhaps not surprising because this type of change is in the Folio regarded as more Irish than Welsh.

Another feature of Fluellen's language is the use of a plural where a singular might be more acceptable in the standard. Where a noun is an object or occurs after a preposition, it may be difficult to decide whether a singular or plural is the more appropriate form. It is only when the plural form of the noun occurs as a subject with the verb in the singular that we can be certain of this Welshism. There are many cases where one or other text has a plural as against the singular in the other text in a non-subject position so that it seems the use of a plural was regarded as significant in some way. The following is a list of examples:

Quarto	Folio	Quarto	Folio
service	services	fauour	Honors
lands	omitted	occasion	occasions
Livings	living	discentions	contention
powers	power	swelling	swellings

Quarto	Folio	Quarto	Folio
mutabilities	mutabilitie	omitted	desires
executions	execution	omitted	requests
disciplines	discipline	omitted	petitions
reconing	reckonings	stomacke	affections
variation	variations	appetite	appetites
tale	tales		

The examples cannot be interpreted with any confidence. More significant are those examples where the noun, when subject, has a plural form with a singular verb. The Folio does increase the number of examples of this failure of concord. What in the quarto had been *your shoes are* and *leekes are* become in the Folio *your shoes is* and *leekes is*. Other examples which have no equivalent in the quarto are also found in the Folio such as *the Mynes is*, noted earlier. Equally when the verb *to be* comes after *there* and a noun follows, there is in the Folio a discrepancy in number not found in the quarto. Hence the quarto *If there be no better direction* becomes in the Folio *if there is not better directions*, and the quarto *There is excellent service* and *thers excellent service* become the Folio *there is very excellent Services* and *there is gallant and most praue passages*. It is evident that in the Folio this usage was regarded as a Welsh feature and every opportunity was taken to introduce it.

However, there are some features of Fluellen's language which are partly or entirely omitted in the Folio despite what had been found in the quarto. When one noun is used as a modifier to another, this in the quarto has what looks like a possessive form with final -*s*. Hence we have *the arrants peece* and *any marshals law*. In the Folio this -*s* is omitted and these forms become *as arrant a piece* and *any marshall law*. Equally characteristic of the quarto is an unusual verbal form. Instead of the third-person singular of a verb, such as *go*, Fluellen uses the third-person singular of the verb *to be* with the infinitive of the lexical verb to give forms like *is go*. There are several examples of this, which I list with the Folio form in brackets: *is maintain* (*keepes*), *is make* (*makes*), *is vtter* (*vtt'red*), *was kill* (*did kill*), *is kill* (*kill*), *is turne away* (*turned away*), *is do* (*fought*), *was do* (*did*), *is strike* (*ha's strooke*), and an example with the first person *I am forget* (*I haue forgot*). Another example, *is come*, is not included, since that is regular in the language of the time and occurs in both quarto and Folio. And one example is found in the Folio which is not in the quarto, namely, *is take* where the quarto has *has tooke*. Also, one example of *is vtter* in the Folio has no equivalent in the quarto. It is clear that this divergent usage made little impression on the editor or compositor of the Folio and so the forms were almost entirely eliminated from the text. Generally, modern editors have followed the Folio in these readings, though there is every reason to suppose that the variant usage was introduced as a marker of Welsh influence in English.

There are a few more points that can be disposed of fairly quickly. In the quarto the word *world* usually appears in Fluellen's speech in the spelling *worell*. In the Folio this is changed either to *world* or to *orld*.[12] The word is either regularised or it is given the more common deviant form in which the initial *w-* is omitted. This variant does occur elsewhere in Shakespeare and that may be a reason for its use in the Folio. There are in the quarto some other variant spellings which I list with the Folio form in brackets: *he hath sed* (*he ha's spoke*), *partition* (*perdition*), *knubs* (*knobs*), *pumples* (not in Folio), *lewer* (perhaps for *lower*, Folio has *fewer*), *Gods sollud* (not in Folio), *frase* (*phrase*), and *knite* (*knight*). It is not certain whether these are misprints or not. Some may well have been intended to suggest a non-standard speaker, though in the Folio Fluellen becomes a man with some Welsh characteristics rather than with substandard speech. Where the quarto has the forms *hath* and *doth*, the Folio replaces them with *ha's* and *doo's*. In one further instance to that already noted the quarto *hee* is replaced by *a*; the example is *hee is vtter* which became *a vtt'red*, and the change may have been inspired by the need to alter the verb form. In general, it seems as though the Folio tends to do away with unusual variant usages and sticks rather to one or two well-known features to represent the Welsh influence on Fluellen's language. Rather than make him non-standard and hence relatively uneducated, the Folio increases the weight of his vocabulary: *desire* replaces *wish*; *contagious* replaces *notablest*, and *bubukles* is introduced. Two or three words may appear as a list in the Folio where there is no equivalent in the quarto like *desires*, *requests*, and *petitions*.

The result of the changes in the Folio is to reduce a dialect speech to one or two characteristic features, which appear frequently, if not regularly. Other deviant usages tend to disappear. Most emphasis is placed on variant spellings indicating a different pronunciation or on particularly striking divergences in syntax. The quarto Fluellen is a non-standard speaker with some traces of Welsh influence in his language; in the Folio he becomes less of a non-standard speaker, but the Welsh features receive more regular treatment.

There are of course in *Henry V* many low-class characters whose speech is substandard. Pistol, Nim, Bardolph, and the Hostess use this type of language. Certain changes between quartos and Folio are worth pointing out. Occurrences of *he* in the quartos are likely to be turned into *a* in the Folio. This applies particularly to Act II, scene iii, in which the final moments of Falstaff are related. However, many of the apparent corruptions of language which appear in the quartos and may have been intended for humour or bawdy or as an indication of an incomplete command of the standard are liable to be eliminated from the Folio. Some of them may indeed have originated as misprints or misunderstandings, though there is no evidence that the Folio reading is more reliable or accurate. The following are part of Pistol's language. The quartos' *Thy mesfull mouth* becomes simply *thy nastie mouth* in the Folio, where *nastie* looks like an attempt to introduce some sense into a phrase that was not understood. In the quartos Pistol says:

> I haue, and I will hold, the quandom quickly,
> For the onely she and Paco, there it is inough.

But the Folio turns *quandom* into *quondam*, and *Paco* into *Pauca*, and so improves his command of Latin. Modern editors follow the Folio here. If it was intended to show that Pistol had scraps of knowledge imperfectly digested, this intention is lost in the Folio and modern editions. Later, when the Hostess wishes to conduct Pistol to Staines, he replies in the quartos *No fur, no fur*. In the Folio this is reduced simply to *No: for my manly heart doth erne*. In the first instance there is an apparent expression of non-standard language, which in the Folio is eliminated to make room for more pompous speech which becomes a take-off of the heroic style fashionable at the time. Later in the same scene Pistol's *cophetua* and *buggle boe* are changed into *Caueto* and *I thee command*. The first word may be a humorous allusion and the second is scatological, but both are changed in the Folio into more acceptable English which has a learned and Latin flavour. In Act III, scene vi, Pistol uses *approach* in the quartos where he means *reproach*, and this may have been intended as a malapropism. It appears as *reproach* in the Folio. In Act IV Pistol refers to the king as a *bago* in the quarto, though this is turned into the more common *Bawcock* in the Folio; and in Act V he says to his French opponent *Eyld cur* in the quarto, but this is turned into *Yeeld Cuure* by the Folio. His final words *home will I trug* in the quarto are not found in the Folio, perhaps because of the non-standard word *trug*. Generally speaking then Pistol's language in the quartos is that of a low-class braggart who mixes up nonsense words and corrupt Latin with slang and vulgar expressions. In the Folio his language has been cleaned up and made less exceptional so that it exemplifies a satire on the pompous and inflated use of the language of the time because much of what he uses would be acceptable in itself were it not found in the wrong context.

A similar reduction of the humorous use of language through corruption or through slang expressions is found in the speech of some other characters. The Hostess says of Falstaff in the quarto that he suffered from *a burning tashan contigian feuer*, a phrase in which the *burning* and *feuer* make clear that the two intermediate words are to be understood as corruptions of medical Latin which was clearly beyond her competence. This is turned into *burning quotidian Tertian* in the Folio. The English of the Folio is less corrupt. Where the Hostess in the quarto refers to *a crysombd childe* the Folio gives this as *any Christome Child*. In these instances and in the examples quoted from Pistol the general tendency in modern editions is to follow the Folio, and this creates a very different feel for the play from what was evidently intended in the quartos.

The quartos have far more ellipsis in the speech of these characters than is found in the Folio. Forms like *sheel* and *ide* in the quartos appear more often as *shee will* and *I would* in the Folio. This does not always occur, however, as the quartos' *of the tide* becomes the Folio *o'th'Tyde*. Asseverations are eliminated or made milder from quarto to Folio. Thus *by gads lugges* becomes simply *by this hand*. The word *push* in the quarto is twice interpreted as *pish* in the Folio. Finally it may be noted in this play that the French of the English low-class speakers like Pistol is much more phonetic in the quarto than in the Folio. His request for identification addressed to the king is *Ke ve la* in the quartos, but that appears as *Che vous la* in the Folio. Equally the French and English spoken by Katherine and Alice are more phonetic in the quarto than the Folio. Thus *han* in the quarto becomes *hand* in the Folio.

We may try now to draw some general conclusions from the small amount of data which has been presented above. We need to distinguish two types of non-standard language: dialect speech and low-class language. The former is much easier to come to terms with. The editors and compositors were able to recognise what was intended as dialect speech and hence they were able to improve upon what was already in their source. This was done by picking up those features which could be recognised as distinctively dialectal and introducing them more thoroughly into the speeches given to the character in question. Less recognisable traits could be omitted. Because dialect speakers were likely to be thought of as non-standard speakers as well, their language could also be given a veneer of colloquialism, though this was not likely to be done in any regular way. Hence dialect speakers became stereotyped, for the audience was given a few clues on a more regular basis. Any other type of humour which may have been intended through this character was likely to be submerged under the general dialect characteristics. Modern editors tend to follow the lead of the Folio in representing the language of dialect speakers, because we too have become acclimatised to certain stock features for each dialect.

Non-standard speakers who have no trace of dialect presented a different and a more difficult problem. It was not clear whether Shakespeare was trying to create a non-standard speaker simply for verisimilitude or whether he was attempting to generate some more specialised form of humour. The character of Pistol is a good example: is he simply a loud-mouthed person who uses low language or is he a stalking-horse through which other contemporary writers could be satirised by having fun poked at their linguistic pretensions? Similarly, is the Hostess to be presented as just a non-standard speaker or is she to be made fun of as a person who introduces malapropisms and other corruptions into her language? The Folio represents a different view of these characters from those found in the quartos and this has put modern editors into a quandary.

Although the text of the Folio may in some plays be more authentic than that of the quartos, it does not follow that the spellings in the Folio had authorial approval. Changes in fashions affecting non-standard language had occurred[13] and would have exercised an influence on the editors and compositors of the Folio. There is a general tendency in the Folio to reduce the amount of variant language on the syntactic and lexical levels. But certain features became associated with non-standard language, such as *a* for *he*, and these features were likely to be introduced into the language of any character who was considered non-standard. Modern editors are more likely to follow the Folio than the quartos, except in those cases where particular features, such as the omission of an article, have been seized upon in certain scenes as indicative of non-standard language. Then these features are likely to be retained in modern editions from the quarto text no matter what is found in the Folio. But this is usually done quite arbitrarily and may depend upon the observations of some nineteenth-century editor which have been handed down. Unless a modern editor is directed in this way to consider some feature of language as significant in the quartos, he is more likely to follow the Folio.

It may also be noted that although many modern editions go in for modern spelling, which means standardising the text in accordance with recognised conventions, there has been no discussion as to what those conventions should be for representing non-standard language.[14] If it is accepted as a convention that non-standard speakers use *a* where standard speakers have *he*, should all examples of the third-person singular masculine personal pronoun in representations of non-standard language be *a* rather than some being *a* and the others *he*? Equally if it is accepted that it is a Shakespearian stage convention that Welsh speakers change the initial labial *b* into *p*, should not all the words which have initial *b-* in Fluellen's speeches be turned into *p-* in modern editions? It would after all not be surprising if an actor pronounced *p* in all these places, because he might wish to present as uniform a language as possible. Why should modern editors draw back from this standardisation? Since they follow the Folio in having more of these examples than were found in the quartos, there seems no reason why they should not carry the procedure to its logical conclusion if their intention is to produce an edition with standardised spelling.

NOTES

1. For a general discussion of non-standard language see N. F. Blake, *Non-standard Language in English Literature* (London: Deutsch, 1981).

2. N. F. Blake, "The Northernisms in *The Reeve's Tale*," *Lore and Language* 3 (1979):1–8.

3. For the Folio, I have used the facsimile edition prepared by Helge Kökeritz (London: Oxford University Press, 1955); for the "1608" quarto the Shakespeare Quarto Facsimiles No. 1 (Oxford: Clarendon Press, 1939); and the ninth edition of Kenneth Muir's *King Lear* (London: Methuen, 1972).

4. The most comprehensive books on Shakespeare's language are Helge Kökeritz, *Shakespeare's Pronunciation* (New Haven: Yale University Press, 1953), and Fausto Cercignani, *Shakespeare's Works and Elizabethan Pronunciation* (Oxford: Clarendon Press, 1981).

5. Kökeritz, 279–80.

6. See A. C. Partridge, *Orthography in Shakespeare and Elizabethan Drama: A Study of Colloquial Contractions, Elision, Prosody and Punctuation* (London: Arnold, 1964).

7. H. Kökeritz, "Elizabethan *Che vor ye* 'I warrant you,' " *Modern Language Notes* 57 (1942):98–103.

8. See S. B. Hemingway, *Henry the Fourth Part I*, A New Variorum Edition of Shakespeare (Philadelphia and London: Lippincott, 1936), 87.

9. G. L. Brook, *The Language of Shakespeare* (London: Deutsch, 1976), says *quotha* "is used sarcastically in repeating something said by another character" (126).

10. See Gary Taylor, *Henry V* (Oxford: Clarendon Press, 1982), Appendix G "Profanities in Q," 316–17.

11. Act III, scene ii, lines 54–60. There is a facsimile in *Henry the Fifth 1600*, Shakespeare Quarto Facsimiles No.9 (Oxford: Clarendon Press, 1957). For quarto and folio see B. Nicholson, *King Henry V: Parallel Texts of the First Quarto (1600) and First Folio (1623) Editions*. New Shakespeare Society (London: Trübner, 1877).

12. Brook, 206.

13. The question of standardisation is discussed by Stanley Wells in his *Re-editing Shakespeare for the Modern Reader* (Oxford: Clarendon Press, 1984).

14. This point is emphasised in Partridge.

Chancery Standard and the Records of Old London Bridge

C. Paul Christianson

In 1977, John Fisher presented, in formal argument, the case for Chancery scribal practices as the dominant influence on the early development of uniform standards for written English. At the time, he wrote:

> During the crucial period between 1420 and 1460, when English first began to be used regularly for government, business, and private transactions, before the advent of printing, and before English had penetrated into the consciousness of the educational establishment, the essential characteristics of Modern Written English were determined by the *practice* of the clerks in Chancery, and communicated throughout England by professional scribes writing in Chancery script, under the influence of Chancery idiom. (Fisher 1977, 898–9)

More recently, when presenting the texts documenting this argument, Fisher has noted the additional texts and data needed to complement the case: "It remains to trace the relationship between the written language of Signet and Chancery, and the written language of the corporations and guilds, the scriveners, and the early printers" (Fisher, Richardson, and Fisher 1984, xvii).

To track the dissemination of Chancery standards for writing during the latter fifteenth century, as we are here invited to do, is a complex task. Among other things, it calls for the identification of many different classes or groups of trained scribes and other professional men of letters, working in London and elsewhere in the country. It also calls for careful scrutiny of these writers' handwriting styles and of the texts they produced, both in Latin and in English, as well as attempts to reconstruct the circumstances of their work and training within various literate communities. Of particular value as evidence in such a general survey would be sets of well-defined archival documents, running the course of many years, and produced under the conditions of a closed shop, such as a record office, where the development of standards for writing and a shift from Latin to English could be traced among a group of identified professional record-keepers. These conditions are in fact well met in the records comprising the archives of the Bridge House Estates, the medieval trust responsible for the administration of old London Bridge. The chief purpose of this essay, therefore, is to examine how well the case for Chancery Standard commends itself by the example of the Bridge trust's small but important record office, whose accounts run continuously throughout the putative period of Chancery influence and whose principal scribes may all be identified.

It has remained a difficult problem to determine, or even to estimate, the number of people who made their living primarily by their literate skills in London and Westminster during the fifteenth century. It is clear, however, that this pool of talent was much larger than often has been imagined, especially if one includes the active members of the Inns of Court and of Chancery. Many in this latter group worked in the offices and courts of the royal administration, there supported by clerical staffs of servants and scribes.[1] If one also includes here the attorneys who came before the royal courts, the numbers approach the "grete multitude" remarked by Caxton in his preface to *The Game of Chess*:

> I suppose that in alle Christendom ar not so many pletars attorneys and men of the lawe as ben in englond onely / for yf they were nombrid all that lange to the courtes of the chancery kinges benche comyn place Chekar ressayt and helle And the bagge berars of the same / hit shold amounte to a grete multitude And how all thyse lyue [and] of whome yf hit shold be vttrid [and] told / hit shold not be beleuyd. (Crotch 1928, 14)

Seen more precisely by one recent count, as many as four hundred of the estimated eleven to twelve hundred members resident in the Inns of Court and of Chancery at any given time after about 1450 were directly involved with professional legal and literate activities, often associated with the government and with its central courts (Baker 1981, 31). In contrast, the civic administration of the City of London, including the principal offices of Common Clerk, Chamberlain, Recorder, and Common Counter, as well as the Mayor, Sheriffs, and Aldermen, required a clerical staff numbering about thirty-five (Orme 1973, 45; Williams 1963, 93–96).

Other groups of professional writers and men of letters are less easily identified by specific places of employment or of residence and training. Within the City, however, it is possible to isolate several groups of writers who gained civic recognition as fraternal misteries of literate craftsmen. Again, the numbers are important to note. For example, London records, at every stage throughout the fifteenth century, point to a sizable body of legal scriveners, many of whom made a living as independent writers serving the mundane legal needs of London citizens by writing and witnessing deeds, wills, and other legal instruments. First organized into a guild of Writers of Court Letter ("Scriptores litterae curialis civitatis Londoniensis") in 1373, these writers were the craft forebears of later members of the Scriveners' Company, royally chartered in 1616–17. Between 1392 and 1500, the names of 210 members and apprentices appear in the guild's *Common Paper* (GL 5370; Steer 1968, vii–viii, 12–13, 20–4). In other instances between 1370 and 1500, the names of at least eighty-five additional writers appear in various London records, identified only as "scryvener" or "scriptor." There is a good possibility that many of these men were also legal writers, although their names do not appear in the guild's archival documents. Additional professional writers served as parish clerks, in London's ninety-nine intramural and eleven extramural churches, who as a group received civic ordinances of organization in 1442 and a royal charter in 1475 (Unwin 1908 [1925], 161, 163).

Associated with the City's book trade were other professional writers, most of whom presumably were members of the Mistery of Stationers, although records of this guild no longer survive. First organized in 1403, the guild united earlier, separate misteries of textwriters and decorative artists (called "limners") and now included bookbinders and booksellers as well; a century and a half later, in 1557, this amalgamated guild of book-craft artisans received a royal charter as the Stationers' Company (Pollard 1937). Artisans involved with book production, it should be noted, were attracted to London in growing numbers from the late fourteenth century onward; between 1370 and 1500, over 260 City stationers and other book craftsmen can now be identified. During the fifteenth century, their numbers during ten-year periods, as indicated in various London records, ranged from a low of thirty-four in the 1420s to a high of fifty in the 1470s, with an average of forty-two per decade. This population, in addition to textwriters, included parchment sellers, bookbinders, and limners, some of whom also worked in writing books produced for the trade (Christianson *Directory* [forthcoming]).

Such professional groups of writers and men of letters, as noted variously here, are exemplary, suggesting the large size of the literate labor force in metropolitan London, especially in the fifteenth century, and pointing to some of the more important divisions within it. Overall, this pool of well-trained talent encompassed a wide social range, from Chancery masters and serjeants-at-law to lowly under-clerks and scribes. Despite vast differences in professional calling, however, it is important to note a demographic factor they shared. To a remarkable extent, the westernmost parishes of the City and the suburbs immediately adjacent to them—the heavily populated Wards of Farringdon Within and Without—had become, even before the fifteenth century, a specialized neighborhood of writers, both legal and literary. The environs of St. Paul's, for example, had emerged, even by the late fourteenth century, as the principal community for manuscript-book production and sale.[2] Similarly, one finds numerous records, dating from this same period, of residence and shop tenancy by legal scriveners in nearby parishes, one account noting that twelve of their members sat each day in the west end of the Cathedral, awaiting business (Simpson 1881, 80).[3] Such common congregation of professional writers within a small, circumscribed area in western London, moreover, was reflected no more than half a mile away near the boundaries of Farringdon Without where Chancery clerks worked in the Rolls Chapel and House or received their apprentice training, first in the *hospicia cancellarie* and later in the lesser Chancery Inns, and where the legal fraternity maintained membership and residence in the greater Inns of Court or the private inns of serjeants and justices (Fisher 1977, 891–92; Richardson 1980, 741–49; Baker 1981, 19).

If in no more than geographic terms, a mutual influence among book-trade writers, legal scriveners, lawyers, and Chancery scribes is a possibility easily imagined. Certainly the area was the center of much literate activity. A portion of the actual day-to-day business of the law and the government, for example, was in fact conducted, not in Westminster, but in City churches and nearby residences. Serjeants-at-law continued to meet daily by the pillars of the "parvis" or porch of St. Paul's, even as they had in Chaucer's day, and attorneys carried on discussions with clients in parish churches in western London, such sites also serving as temporary repositories for many of the current rolls and writs of the central courts (Hastings 1947 [1971], 38–39). One must also imagine the activities of legal scriveners, many of whom hung samples of their writings outside their small shops to attract customers, but who also frequently sought or conducted scribal work in nearby taverns. Book artisans, in turn, were regular visitors to the shops of fellow craftsmen, in the course of shared labor on book commissions (Christianson *Directory* [forthcoming]). Within the same quarter, one would also have been aware of student or scholarly life, in the City grammar schools at St. Paul's, St. Martin-le-Grand, and St. Mary-le-Bow, in the cathedral school of St. Paul's, and in the *studia generalia* of the London convents—Greyfriars, Blackfriars, and Whitefriars (Courtenay 1985, 128–32).

If indeed, as Fisher has argued, a growing prestige attached to Chancery and its clerks eventually set a precedent for styles of handwriting and for standard forms in written English texts, such a possibility is more readily seen in a flourishing neighborhood of well-trained writers, as presently described. It would appear, moreover, that one place to look for the early stages of Chancery influence would be here, in this socially complex but lively community of literate talent. An example to be mooted may in fact be found among writers drawn from this community, the scribes responsible for the extensive records of London Bridge whose "office standard" for writing in the Bridge House may be traced throughout the fifteenth century.

To introduce the Bridge records and the men who wrote them, one must begin by commenting briefly on old London Bridge itself. Until 1750, when Westminster Bridge was opened, London Bridge was the sole span across the Thames in the metropolitan area. Its construction had begun in 1176, and the final stonework was completed thirty-three years later, in 1209. From the outset, this magnificent structure was the particular pride of many London citizens, and the Bridge's maintenance and administration were soon made the City's responsibility. To that end, even in the thirteenth century before the legal form of trusts had completely evolved, a City of London charity was established, still in existence today and now known as the Bridge House Estates Trust, to solicit gifts of endowment and to oversee the Bridge as a civic institution (Masters 1972, [1–2]; Jones 1953, 59–60). Overall responsibility for Bridge maintenance and management of its many enterprises, including the rental of numerous London properties acquired through donors' gifts, lay with two Wardens or Proctors, who after 1311 were elected annually by the Commonalty (Williams 1963, 87). Such wardenship, throughout the Bridge's early history, was often held by prominent London citizens.[4] As early as the thirteenth century, the Wardens' administrative duties came to be centered in a special building constructed for these purposes, called the Bridge House. This structure was located in Southwark, to the east of the Bridge end, north of Tooley Street (Masters 1972, [3]).

To meet the demands of the Bridge itself while managing the trust's growing property endowment, the Bridge Wardens employed a special staff of salaried clerks as well as numerous workmen. The principal officer working under the Wardens was known as the Clerk of the Works, and he, in turn, had other clerks under

his supervision.[5] The earliest direct documentation of this division
of labor within the Bridge House dates to 1381, in the first set of
extant annual accounts drawn up by the Clerk, although it is clear
that in some form an organization of clerical staff had developed
much earlier.[6] After 1381, the annual accounts continue, year by
year, to 1500 (and beyond). What is of greatest value in them, for
purposes of this essay, is the unbroken record of dated salary payments for the Bridge Clerks, providing exact years of tenure for
these men and allowing a clear identification of their handwriting
during the various years of their clerkship. These ten Clerks of
the Works and their tenure dates are as follows:

> William Aston (1381–82 to 1404–5)
> John Hethingham (1405–6 to 1420–21)
> Thomas Hakun (1421–22 to 1427–28)
> John Speldsell (1428–29 to 1439–40)
> Robert Blome (1440–41 to 1442–43)
> John Parker (1443–44 to ?1444–45)
> John Elys (?1445–46 to ?1459–60)[7]
> William Bouchier (1460–61 to 1481–82)
> John Pays (1482–83 to 1487–88)
> John Normavyle (1488–89 to 1501–2).

As reported in the accounts, the activities of these Clerks suggest that a degree of familiarity with legal forms was required in
meeting the duties of their office. A Clerk's responsibilities included writing weekly accounts of receipts and expenditures for
the Bridge and its enterprises; preparing engrossed copies of the
accounts in an abridged form for purposes of annual audit; drawing up indentures, bonds, deeds, and other legal instruments on
behalf of the Wardens; and representing the Bridge when required
in actions in the secular courts. As full-time writers in a busy
record office, these Clerks and the many records they wrote thus
offer an unusual opportunity to trace the development of an office
standard for writing.

The medieval documents in the Bridge House archives, which
are of concern here, fall into two main categories: muniments and
annual accounts. A series of ancient deeds, now indexed as ten
portfolios lettered A through K, covers a number of the more than

eight hundred properties in London and surrounding communities acquired by the Bridge trust, most of them received before 1600. In the late fifteenth century, these deeds and others that no longer survive were copied in a small register, a process that was repeated in 1513–14, in a large, handsomely produced register, written by the talented legal scrivener John Halmer (Christianson 1987). The other principal Bridge records are the annual accounts prepared by the Clerk of the day, the earliest of which survive in seventeen parchment rolls covering the period 1381–98 and 1404–5. After 1404, the records appear in a different format, shifting to weekly journals, written on loose paper quires, which were eventually bound into books. One such book recorded weekly expenditures and the other, weekly receipts. The earliest series of expenditures covers the period 1404–45 and was originally bound in four volumes, all extant. The alternate set of journals, those recording receipts, covers the period 1404–60, preserved in two original volumes. After 1460, the surviving records are found in the form of abridged accounts specially prepared annually for the Bridge auditors. Carefully written each year by the Clerk, these vellum quire copies were periodically collected and bound into large volumes for deposit in the Guildhall. The first two books in this series cover the period 1460–1509.[8]

The Clerks' handwriting in the yearly dated accounts provides extensive evidence over a period of 120 years of scribal practice in record-keeping within the control of the Bridge House office. Generally speaking, the records show a growing familiarity with—and by the early 1440s an apparently deliberate adoption of—the cursive form of handwriting known now as Secretary Script. Increasingly in the fifteenth century, this new script came to displace for many London writers that older cursive script that had become common to many fourteenth-century books and records—and which is now named Anglicana by M. B. Parkes (Parkes 1969 [1979], xiv–xvi; xix–xxi). The transition in the Bridge records is marked by a mixture of graph forms of the two scripts. The Bridge Clerks' shift from Latin to English as the language of official record was somewhat later in coming, not completed until the accounts for 1480, although an extended passage in English occurs eleven years earlier, in records for 1467–68, written on 23 January 1469–70.

The earliest evidence of the use of Secretary graphs in the Bridge records is found in accounts written by Thomas Hakun, Clerk of the Works between 1421–22 and 1427–28. Both of his predecessors, William Aston and John Hethingham, had written consistently in Anglicana Script.[9] A similar preference for Anglicana, but now to a degree influenced by the angularity of Secretary graphs, characterizes the hands of Hakun's successors, John Speldsell (1428–29 to 1439–40) and Robert Blome (1440–41 to 1442–43). Unfortunately, little can be learned about these earliest Clerks, especially about the circumstances of their training as writers. One can only infer from their handwriting that such training had been careful and demanding. Hakun, for example, was a somewhat meticulous writer, even when writing rapidly (a feature of all surviving Bridge records before 1460), and he was also skilled in finely drawn decorative penwork (BHE 1421–30, fols. 30, 74, 114, 157). Throughout the many pages of records he wrote, his handwriting is normally compact and evenly formed. Among the Secretary graphs he favored are the single-compartment a and both the broken-stem and 2-shaped r. There is a tendency too toward more angular formation of letters, at times with slight horns appearing. These latter features, however, were characteristic of mixed Anglicana and Secretary texts at the time, and it would be fair to say that until 1443 Anglicana Script remained the commonly used (and perhaps preferred) office standard within the Bridge House.

For reasons yet to be determined, such an office standard appears to have shifted somewhat deliberately during the tenure of the next two Clerks, John Parker (1443–44 to ?1444–45) and John Elys (?1445–46 to ?1459–60). In contrast to his predecessor, Parker wrote his accounts in a well-formed hand in which Secretary graphs now are common. Among these are the single-compartment a; a broken-stroke r; horned e; t with its shaft well above the headstroke; angular lobes on b and d; and a pointed, single-compartment g. Minims are also clearly formed. A similar commitment to a style of handwriting increasingly based on

Secretary Script is found in Parker's successor, John Elys, whose hand appears as early as 1444 in the records and is found intermittently in entries to 1460. Notable among Elys's preferred graph forms are the Secretary horned *e*, *c*, *o* and *g*; single-compartment *a*; bent b-form *s*; *w* now formed as two *v*'s. In many instances, letters are shaped by strongly angular strokes.

Can one account for this sudden shift in writing style? A partial answer may lie in data that survive about these two Clerks. Parker's scribal background can be clearly identified. He was a legal scrivener, recently admitted to the Mistery of Writers of Court Letter, on 28 June 1442 (Steer 1968, 22). He was, subsequently, to have a long and very busy career in London as a legal writer; as late as 1490, he was still active in guild affairs (Steer 1968, 11–13, 22–24; Christianson 1987). Parker would have brought to the office of Clerk the virtues of his training, which, among members of his guild, took the form of strict apprenticeship in scriveners' shops. No records survive identifying Parker's master, but his education may have been a family affair. Another John Parker, perhaps his grandfather, who died in 1401, was also a scrivener (GL 9171/1 (Courtney), 468). This earlier Parker was probably the scribe of London, Lincoln's Inn MS Hale 187, a set of year books subsequently owned by the later Parker's colleague, the scrivener William Brampton (Ker 1969, 139; Steer 1968, 11–12, 20–21). John Parker's father may also have been named John, for in 1412, a John Parker rented a shop in West Cheap, near St. Paul's, presumably the same property that, in 1457, the later Parker is identified as once having owned (Chew 1965, 77; CCR 1454–61, 159). In 1432, this earlier John Parker had association with the stationer Bartholomew Fraunceys, perhaps an indication that he too was a professional writer (CCR 1429–35, 312–13).

As for John Elys, it would appear that he was a textwriter in the manuscript-book trade in London, presumably the John Elys, late of the parish of St. Peter upon Cornhill, who in his will of 1467 was identified as citizen, "stacioner," and "haberdasher" (GL 9171/6 (Wilde), 12). As this will notes, Elys was a brother of the limner William Elys; later, between 1475 and 1483, William Elys

was a tenant in a shop in Old Chaunge, the small lane directly east
of St. Paul's churchyard (BHA 1460–84, 250, 265 *et passim*).
There is also a good possibility that the two Elys brothers were
related to the limner and stationer Richard Elys, also a tenant in
a Bridge-owned shop located in Paternoster Row, directly north
of the Cathedral churchyard, which he held between 1460 and
1470 (BHA 1460–84, 3, 21v *et passim*). If this identification of
John Elys is correct, then he would have brought to his clerkship
of the Bridge scribal habits learned from professional and family
associations in the close-knit community of the City's book trade
(Christianson *Directory* [forthcoming]).

The consistent use of Secretary Script by both Parker and Elys
in writing Bridge records during the 1440s and 1450s may well
indicate a more general acceptance of this style of writing among
London's legal scriveners and book-trade writers at the time.[10] To
an extent, this surmise is borne out by the evidence of contemporary texts. In the case of legal scriveners, the clearest documentation of a shift in writing style is to be found in the guild's
Common Paper where, after 1440, Secretary Script becomes the
predominant model used by new members when writing their
declarations, upon admission to the mistery (Parkes 1969 [1979],
xxi, n1). Parker's own skill in writing Secretary, even at the outset
of his career, may be seen in the declaration he wrote in 1442
(GL 5370, 71). Further evidence of the transition in scripts occurring may be found in two entries recording petitions made by the
scriveners before the Mayor and Aldermen (see Plate 1, A and
B). The first petition dates from 1439–40, and its text is written in a combination of Anglicana and Secretary. By the time of
the second petition, written in 1449–50, a shift to Secretary is
now complete. The widespread acceptance of this change by the
guild's members, moreover, is indicated by the close congruity of
handwriting in the statements of support for this petition, supplied
by nineteen scriveners (see Plate 2). John Parker was part of this
group, all of whom were prominent members of the guild.[11] In
virtually every instance, a mastery of Secretary Script is clearly
evident.

Unfortunately, comparable guild records for the Mistery of Stationers no longer survive, and one is forced to look elsewhere for textual evidence showing a similar turn to Secretary Script among those writing literary works. Earlier in the century, the example of Thomas Hoccleve, who was one of five scribes writing Cambridge, Trinity College MS R.3.2 (581), Gower's *Confessio Amantis*, stands in contrast to the other scribes' work. The stints contributed by his fellow writers, many if not most of whom may have been members of the Mistery of Stationers, were written in versions of Anglicana, whereas Hoccleve wrote in the Secretary Script he had mastered as a Privy Seal clerk (Doyle and Parkes 1978). On the basis of other surviving texts of Gower, Chaucer, and Lydgate, now found in the Bodleian Library, Parkes has suggested that the appearance of Secretary Script in such manuscripts was more typical of book production during the second half of the fifteenth century than during the first half (Parkes 1969 [1979], xxi, n1). Examples closer to the middle of the century are found in London texts written or annotated by the amateur scribe and book enthusiast, John Shirley (d. 1456), although his use (but hardly mastery) of Secretary forms in his old age (e.g., London, Sion College MS Arc. L 40.2/E.44; Ker 1969, 290–91; cf. Parkes 1978, 10) may have developed much earlier, in his career as secretary to the Earl of Warwick. A more significant example would appear to be that found in San Marino, Huntington Library MS HM 39465, an astronomical miscellany written throughout in a version of Secretary (see Plate 3). This manuscript's tie to commercial book production in London mid-century seems to be signaled by the occurrence of the scribe's name, "R. Elys," or his initials three times in the volume (fols. 18v, 30, 44v). There is a good possibility that this Elys was the stationer and limner Richard Elys, cited earlier in connection with John Elys. Among London records examined, the earliest reference to Richard Elys, "stacioner," dates to 1455, when he agreed, along with two other stationers, John Bryght and William Dawbeney, to submit their quarrel to arbitration (JCCC 5, 246v). In 1459, Richard Elys was mentioned in the will of the stationer Robert Chirche (GL 9171/5 (Sharp), 281), and in 1461, he had association with the stationer Nicholas Silverton (CPMR 1458–82, 158). Clearly, this

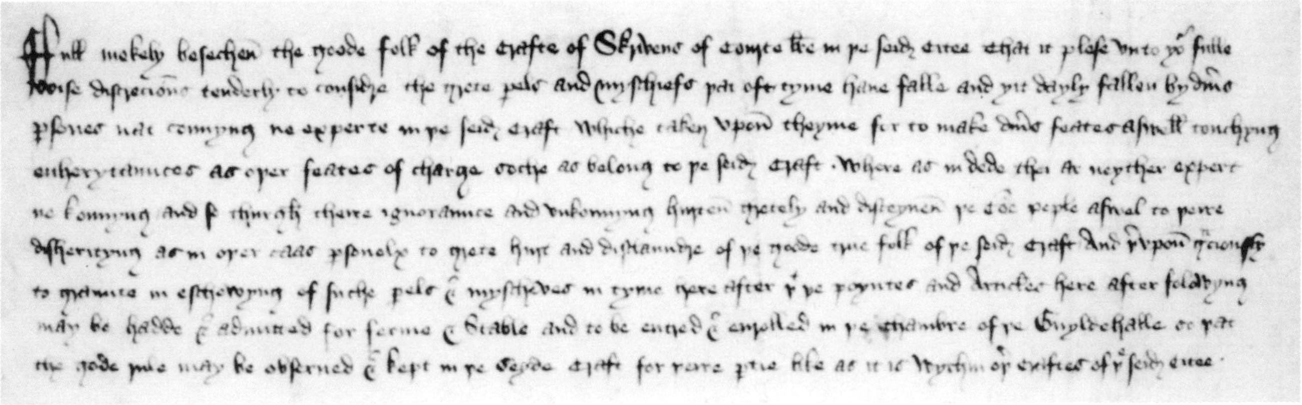

Plate I (A). London, Guildhall Library MS 5370 Scriveners' Company Common Paper, p. 9 (13 January 1439–40). Detail. Original page size approximately 292 x 394 mm.

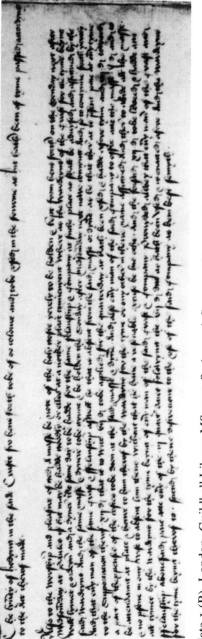

Plate 1 (B). London, Guildhall Library MS 5370 *Scriveners' Company Common Paper*, p. 15 (18 April 1449–50). Detail. Original page size approximately 292 x 394 mm.

Plate 2. London, Guildhall Library MS 5370 *Scriveners' Company Common Paper*, p. 15 (18 April 1449–50). Detail. Original page size approximately 292 x 394 mm.

Richard Elys was part of the City book-trade community. Perhaps of greater significance, the scribe's handwriting in Huntington MS HM 39465 shares certain similarities in its use of Secretary Script to that of John Elys in contemporary Bridge records. Such cursory evidence as here outlined, if it does not misrepresent the case, points to a developing interest in Secretary Script among legal and literary writers working in London during the 1440s and 1450s. The question remains, however, did the adoption of a new script arise because of an increased use of Secretary among Chancery scribes prominent in the scribal community, beginning in the 1430s, as noted by Fisher (Fisher, Richardson, and Fisher 1984, 5)? Before attempting to answer this question, one must turn to other complementary evidence available, that of English-language texts written in Secretary Script during this period.

Appropriate examples to be cited here are the petitions made by the legal scriveners to the Mayor and Aldermen, noted earlier, as found in the *Common Paper*. To what extent are the written forms of English in these entries comparable to those then developing in Chancery-related texts? A transcription of the opening portion of the first of these petitions, dated 13 January 1439–40, reads as follows (see Plate 1, A):

> Full mekely besechen the goode folk of the Crafte of Skrivens of Courte *lett*re in the seid' Citee That it plese vnto yo*ur* fulle wise descrecions tenderly to considre the grete p*er*els and myschiefs þat oft tyme haue falle and yit dayly fallen by diu*er*s p*er*sones nat connyng ne experte in þe seid' Craft Whiche taken vpon' theyme for to make diu*er*s feates aswell' touchyng enherytannces [?enherytaunces] as oþer feates of charge soche as belong to þe seid' Craft. Where as in dede thei ar neyther expert ne konnyng and so thurgh' theire ignorannce [?ignoraunce] and vnkonnyng hurten' gretely and disceyuen' the Co*mo*ne peple aswel to þeire disherityng as in oþer caas p*er*sonele*s* to grete hurt and disclanndre [?disclaundre] of þe goode true folk of þe seid' Craft / And þervpon' graciously to grannte [?graunte] in eschewyng of suche p*er*eles & Myscheves in tyme here after þat þe poyntes and Articles here after folowyng may be hadde & admitted for ferme & Stable

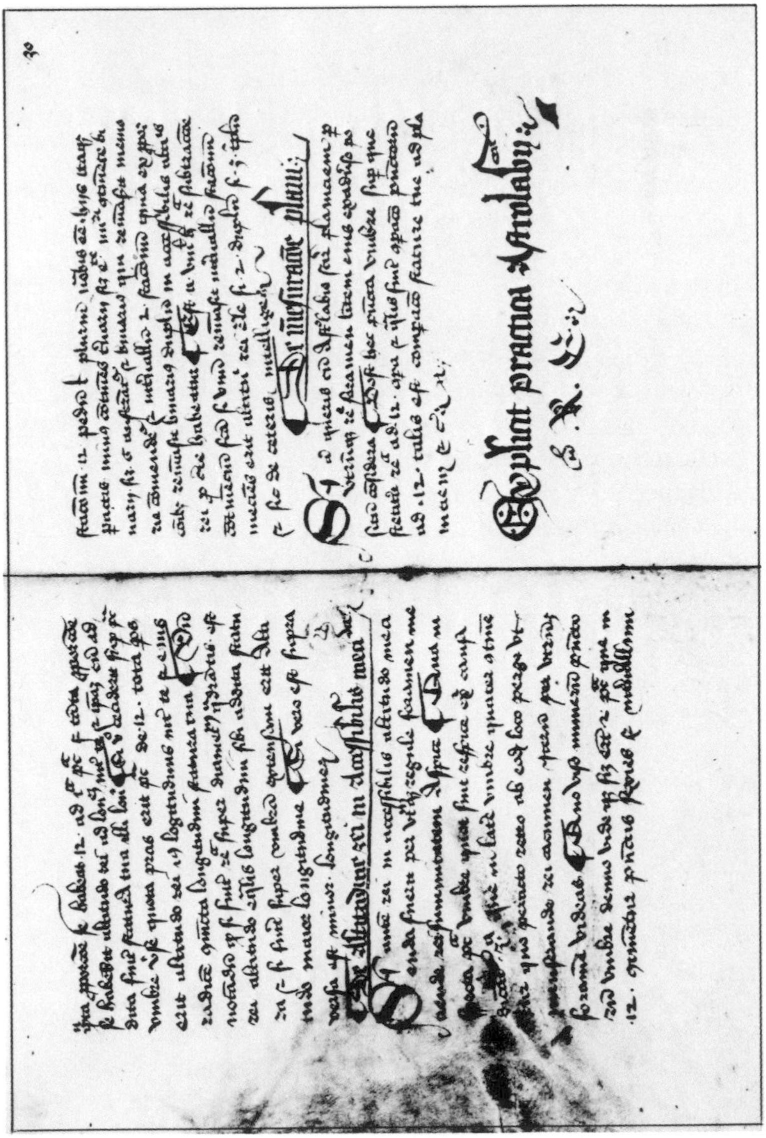

Plate 3. San Marino, California, Huntington Library MS HM 39465 *Astronomical Miscellany*, fols. 29v–30. s. xv med. Original page size approximately 105 x 146 mm.

and to be entred & enrolled in þe Chambre of þe Guyldehalle so
þat the gode rule may be obserued & kept in þe Seyde Craft for
þeire p*ar*tie like as it is Wythin oþ*er* Craftes of þe seid' Citee.

Examination of this passage reveals, in a number of instances,
forms for writing the vernacular that parallel those coming into
common use in Chancery documents from the late 1430s and that
were to become features of a Chancery standard:[12] spellings for
whiche and *suche/soche* and the use of *gh* in *thurgh*; the third-
person plural pronoun as *thei/theire/theyme*; the ending *ly* on
adverbs, such as *mekely, tenderly, dayly, gretely, graciously*; the
present participle ending *yng*, as in *touchyng, konnyng*; the past
participle ending *ed*, as in *admitted, entred, enrolled, obserued*;
the use of the prefix *en* where modern spelling would be *in*, as
in *enherytannces*. Certain non-Chancery forms are also present,
although all are found as exceptional forms in Chancery-related
documents: *nat* (instead of *not*); *ar* (instead of *be/been*); *seid*
(instead of *said*); and the use of *en* as the plural verb inflection,
as in *taken, hurten, disceyuen*.

For purposes of comparison, the second scriveners' petition,
written ten years later and dated 18 April 1449–50, may be cited
(see Plate 1, B). A transcription of the opening portion of this
petition reads as follows:

> The lyu*er*ey of hodyng in the saide Crafte fro hens forth tobe of oo
> coloure and' tobe vsed' in the fourme as hit hath' been of tyme
> passed accordyng to the Act therof made.

> Also to the Worship' and pleasire of god' A masse be note of the
> holy goste yerely to be holden & kept from hens forth' on the
> Sonday next after Midsom*er*day at Paules if hit may be hadde
> goodly or elles at a nother place conuenyent Where as the Wardeyns
> of the Craft for the tyme beyng will lymet & ordeyn' and a dyner'
> the same day to be hadde for the same felauship' & Company at
> suche place as shall be aduysed and assigned by the said'
> Wardeyns. And' the same masse & dynere tobe gynne & be holden
> the Sonday after Midsom*er*day next nowe comyng. And' so to
> contynue forth yerely. And that eu*er*y man of the same Craft &
> Felauship' aswell he that is absent from the said' masse or dyn*er* as
> he that ther*e* at is pr*e*sent paie at eu*er*y tyme to the Supportacion

therof. xij. d'. that is to Wite. vij d'. tobe applied for the quarterday
as hath been used & hadde afore tyme and iiij. d' toward' a part of
thexpenses of the costes tobe doon at the said' masse & dyner. And
also euery man of the said' Company to offre atte the masse. j. d'
and to be attendannt [?attendaunt] at place & houre to him therof by
the Wardeyns for the tyme or ony other' in theire name assigned.
And ther' to abide att the masse & no persone in ony wise to absent
him thens without that he haue a resonable excuse be his othe. And
the forsaid xij. d' tobe leveed' & hadde atte all tymes by the
Wardeyns for the tyme beyng of euery man of the said' Craft &
Company Prouyded alwey that euery man of the Craft and
Felaushi p' abouesaid' paie atte euery of the iij quarter Daies
folowyng the vij. d' due as hath been vsed & is enacted' afore. And
the Wardeyns for the tyme beyng therof to spend' by theire
Discrecions to the vse of the said' Company as hem best semyth.

Here, as in the preceding petition, certain written forms appear
to be standardized and to have become so in ways comparable to
Chancery practices. Examples include adverbs in *ly*, as in *yerely*,
goodly; the present participle in *yng*, as in *comyng*, *folowyng*;
the past participle in *ed*, as in *aduysed*, *assigned*, *applied*; the
third-person singular inflection, present tense, as *hath*, *semyth*;
the suffix *cion*, as in *Supportacion*, *Discrecions*; the double *o*, as
in *doon* and *oo* (for *oon*). Certain non-Chancery forms remain,
however, as in the spelling of *ony* (instead of *eny/any*) and of *be*
(instead of *by*) or in the writing of *tobe* as a single word. Chancery *fro* alternates with non-Chancery *from*. In syntactic terms,
moreover, this passage appears to favor, even more so than the petition of 1439–40, a phrasal orientation to a curial style of writing
that was also a distinctive feature of Chancery-related documents
(Burnley 1986). Notable elements in this style, the goal of which
was primarily that of coherence and clarity of reference, include
the use of doublets (as in the phrases *to be holden & kept*; *will
lymet & ordeyn*; *shall be aduysed and assigned*; *as hath been used
& hadde*) and anaphoric determiners (as in the phrases *the same
felauship & Company*; *the same masse & dynere*; *the said Craft &
Company*; *the Craft and Felaushi p abouesaid*; *the said Wardeyns*;
the forsaid xij d).

If we return to the question of influence by Chancery-trained scribes, the evidence here provided by the scriveners' petitions of 1439–40 and 1449–50 suggests a parallel movement toward writing standards on the part of both groups that is more than coincidental. Moreover, the size of the Chancery staff and the prominence of its chief Clerks, both in the community of London writers and in government affairs, would seem to imply the more powerful influence of Chancery practices, here beginning to be acknowledged among members of a small London guild of professional writers. By extension, such growing influence may also have been felt among textwriters in the book trade. If this was so, then the lead established by Chancery scribes may have been acknowledged south of the river as well, by legal and literary writers such as John Parker and John Elys and by their successors composing the Bridge House records.

The decision finally to shift from Latin to English as the language of record within the Bridge House was relatively late in coming, not occurring until 1480 (BHA 1460–84, 310 ff.). The Clerk responsible for this radical change was William Bouchier, whose tenure ran from 1460–61 to 1481–82. As indicated earlier, the Bridge records that survive from the last forty years of the fifteenth century are the abridged summaries of annual accounts specially prepared for purposes of an annual audit. In contrast to the earlier records of income and expenditure, these later abridgements were artfully written, with close attention paid to their presentation. All are written in a more formal version of Secretary Script, and each successive Clerk shows a mastery of this style of handwriting. The office standard for record production extended, moreover, to the written forms of English, once the decision had been made to change the language of record. Overall, the Bridge House standards for English composition followed by Bouchier and by his successors, John Pays (1482–83 to 1487–88) and John Normavyle (1488–89 to 1501–2), match well the written standards for Chancery English operating at the time. Such congruity may be illustrated in sample passages written by these Clerks of the Works.

The first extended passage in English in the Bridge accounts occurs at the end of the records for 1467–68 and is dated 23 January 1469–70, much earlier than the actual shift to English in the records. Bouchier's entry deals with the auditors' complaint about the expenses of the Wardens' horses. The opening portion of this passage reads as follows:

> This acounte was herde & finisshid the xxiij day of Januar in the ixth yere of the regne of Kynge Edward the fourth by the auditours within wreten Whiche vnder stondyng that afore tyme ther was a carte and horses ther to bilongyng kepte atte gretter costes of the same Brugge than the profits growyng by cariage made by the same Whiche was shewid and declarid vnto the meyre and aldermen of this cite And therupon by the advise of the Courte It was ordeyned that the seyde carte and horses shuld be putte awey and the maisters of the brugge for the tyme beyng to pay for alle maner cariage longyng to the seide Brugge Werkes acordyng to ther iourneys Whiche was founde after grete profite to the seide Brugge. (BHA 1460–84, 144v)

For purposes of comparison, another of Bouchier's entries may be cited, written eleven years later in the accounts for 1480, at the time when the language of record had turned exclusively to English. The passage outlines the auditors' restrictions on the board supplied to Bridge workmen:

> We understonding and knowing that Walter Reve wardeyn of the Carpentry of the Bridge and diverse of his feleship carpenters and the masons kepe a comyns of bordemen within the Bridgehous of the whiche one is wekely styward and purveour and daily biethe and dressith ther mete taking his wages hoole of the Cite and also spendyng woode and fewell of the places stuffe in sethyng and rostyng ther viteles and there laborers attending the same The seide auditours consideryng the coste and charge that the Cite hath be putte in tyme passid and dailly is putte to by mene of the same comyns in spendyng of wode and fewell and also wages as is aforeseide they have utterly determyned and ordeyned that from Sonday next comyng which shalbe the seconde day of September that the seide Carpenters nor the Mason kepe comyns and bordemen within the Bridgehous but they to have loggyng within

the place to thentent that they and everych of hem shalbe redy bothe
by day and by night yf any jeparde and casualte of hurte falle atte
Bridge or with in the place. (BHA 1460–84, 321; Jones 1953, 62)

Both of these passages show Bouchier's consistent use of English forms that were preferred, and by this date increasingly
standardized, in Chancery writing. In morphology, Bouchier em-
ploys *they, ther, hem* for the plural pronoun, third person; *whiche*
as relative; *this* as demonstrative. The past participle is formed
with *d*, as in *herde, finisshid, shewid, declarid, ordeyned*; the
third-person singular inflection, present tense, occurs as *requir-
eth, biethe, dressith*; adverbs are regularly formed with *ly* (*fully,
wekely, daily, utterly*). Bouchier's writing also shares certain features of Chancery orthography; at times, his spellings concur with
those often idiosyncratic forms found in Chancery documents,
e.g., *o* before *n* (*understondyng*); *e* in *show* and *move* (*shewid,
mevid*). Certain differences from Chancery practices also occur
(e.g., *from*, not *fro*; *one*, not *oon*; the use of genitive inflection with inanimate nouns, as in *brugges coste*; *places stuffe*), but
overall an apparent familiarity with Chancery forms is evident.

Bouchier's successor as Clerk of the Works was John Pays (also
spelled Pees), a legal scrivener who was admitted to the Mistery
of Writers of Court Letter on 6 August 1469. Pays had received
his training from a Richard Pays, presumably his father or blood
relative, who had been admitted to the guild in 1457 (Steer 1968,
22). Like Bouchier, Pays was a highly skilled writer whose command of Secretary Script is almost completely assumed in the texts
he wrote for the Bridge during his tenure (1482–88). Likewise,
Pays's command of English matches well that of contemporary
Chancery clerks, as may be seen in a passage outlining expenses
of the Chapel of St. Thomas á Becket, located on the Bridge itself.
A portion of this entry, from 1486–87, reads as follows:

Item paide vnto . . . Robert Tye of reward to hym allowed for
kepyng of the organs and for his diligent attendaunce in openyng
and shuttyng the Chapel doris and kepyng the goodes and
ornamentes of the seid Chapell w^tynne the tyme of this accompte
xx*s* And to the preestes and clerkes syngyng placebo and diryge and

masses of requiem for the soulis of alle the benefactours of the
Brigge iiij tymes this yere viij*s* And for wasshyng of Awbys Amyces
Awterclothes surplices Towels and other ornamentes belongyng to
the seid Chapell iiij*s* And to William Mylet Wexchaundeler for
Tapers and candelles ayenst cristmas Candilmas and for the pascall
Judas candille and the beme lyght ayenst the Fest of translacion of
Seint Thomas as it apperith by his bill xxviij*s* j*d* Item paide to
Richard Alphegh for ix galons oyle spendid in the lampe and in the
lampis of the braunche w^tout the chapell dore atte seid Fest of seint
Thomas x*s* vj*d* Item paide to John Barell Stacioner for the
amendyng of certeyn bokes w^tyn the seid place and settyng in newe
quayres in to them as more playnly it appereth by his bill xxvj*s* x*d*
Item for xv *lb* Talowe candell spended in the same chapell in doyng
dyuine seruice in wynter tyme this yere xv*d* Item paide for the
amendyng of a surples iiij*d*. (BHA 1484–1509, 54)

Here, once again, one finds the consistent use of many preferred
Chancery forms for English: the past participle with *d*, even in
instances where Modern English would be different (*spendid*);
the third-person singular inflection, present tense, as in *apperith*; the idiosyncratic personal pronoun phrase, *euery of them*; the
preposition *ayenst*. Also notable is the use of the gerund with
yng, including the verb *do* here used as a causative main verb
(*doyng dyuine seruice*; *kepyng*; *openyng and shuttyng*; *wasshyng*;
amendyng).

The apparent standard for writing English accounts within the
Bridge House, as indicated in the records produced by Bouchier
and Pays, continued in the productions of the last Clerk here to
be considered, John Normavyle (1488–1502). In his writings for
the Bridge, Normavyle represents the highest calling among the
successive Clerks in terms both of his skills in handwriting and
his standards for uniform English. Throughout his tenure, Normavyle's hand exhibits a remarkably consistent presentation of a
well-formed Secretary Script. From entry to entry and from year
to year, there is little variation in his expert execution. Normavyle
also had considerable calligraphic skills, which he used to enhance
the clear writing of his texts through the addition of bold and flam-
boyant penwork. Such decoration frequently involved elaborate

cadels and grotesques and occasionally incorporated figure draw-
ings of heraldic beasts and birds, some of them copied from early
printed playing cards or model sheets based on them.[13] Equally
controlled was Normavyle's command of English, with consistent
preferences for spelling uniformity apparent in his accounts from
early to late. A typical passage occurs in the accounts for 1501–2,
a portion of which shows the variety of payments made by the
Bridge Wardens for "Expencis Necessary." These include, among
many others, the costs of lawsuits, of cleaning ordure from la-
trines, of repairing boats and tenements, and of taking down the
pageant used in welcoming Catherine of Aragon at her royal entry
into London at the Bridge:

> To Tharchebisshop of Caunterbury and to the priour of the
> Charterhous at Sheane for sute to their Courtes in Suthwerk and
> leuesham Sum iij*s* to John Poynte attourney of the Common place
> in sute of henry Bumstedes obligacione with his Fee for this
> instante yere xiij*s* xj*d* to John Bysset John Saddeler and William
> Marchall for voydyng of iiij*ˣˣ* xvij Tonne of Order oute of dyuers
> and sundry tenementes this yere takyng for euery Tonne xx*d* Sum
> viij*li* xx*d* to the same John and John for spredyng serchyng and
> clensyng of iij other Seges x*s* to Robert Wakeryng and John
> Crowchman attendyng nightely vpon the sayd voiders and to
> nombre the tonnes iiij*s* viij*d* to William Rodley of Depford for
> reparaciones doon there at the signe of the Cristopher soo letten to
> hym at taxe by the ouersight of the Bridgemaisters vj*s* viij*d* . . . To
> William Snowden for corieng and repairyng of botes belongyng to
> the said bridgehouse vj*s* to the same William for takyng downe of
> the pagent of london bridge at taxe x*s* And for expencis upon the
> masons and Carpenters the day of the entre of the lady princes for
> their Watche and delygente attendaunce geven by theym vnto the
> same xj*s*. (BHA 1484–1509, 224v)

In all his many writings for the Bridge, of which this passage is
illustrative, Normavyle equaled and in certain respects surpassed
the writing of Chancery clerks who were contemporary with him,
both in mastery of script and in uniformity of English forms.
His achievements exemplify well the high level of scribal performance now expected of Bridge Clerks and the formal standards

for record-keeping that had clearly evolved in the Bridge House office. Such tradition of excellence was to continue in the sixteenth century. Normavyle's successor as Clerk was the stationer Walter Smyth, himself an able writer, who had working for him during his tenure (1502–3 to 1522–23) the exceptionally talented legal scrivener John Halmer, who in 1514 wrote the large register of deeds of Bridge properties, 666 entries in all, each decorated by elaborate penwork cadels, heraldic figures, and freehand drawing of foliage designs (Christianson 1987). Smyth, in turn, was succeeded by an equally talented writer, John Halmer's son, also named John Halmer, who, like his father, was a member of the Mistery of Writers of Court Letter (Steer 1968, 12, 23, 25).

Although little survives in the Bridge accounts to indicate what the various Clerks of the Works thought of their scribal work, it may be said of John Normavyle, at least, that he considered recognition of his achievements as something due him. His ambition for success as a writer is reflected in the special reward of £6 13s 4d he received in 1496 for meritorious work (this sum in addition to his annual salary of £10 and his fee of 66s 8d for writing and doubling the account books). Normavyle's professional pride in scribal work, moreover, is evident in the commendation of his labor, which he himself wrote into the year's account and probably composed:

> And to the same John of a speciall Rewarde to him allowed for his
> good and diligent attendaunce daily in his office In forberyng alle
> other Werkis and besynes and oonly attendyng vnto the same And
> in thabsence of the said Wardeyns alwey redy abiding and
> ouerseyng the Werkemen & laborers werkyng in the said bridge
> worke for the great spede of the same werkis Also duely
> countrollyng the beryng onto & bryngyng yn of alle maner stuf and
> ordenance pertynyng to the same Werkis And the Remaynder therof
> entryng & declaryng in thende of this present booke And in alle
> other thingis concernyng his said office Duely employng his Wittes
> and diligence to the most availe & profaite of this place And workis
> of the same this yere. (BHA 1484–1509, 180)

An equal measure of pride taken in the quotidian work of a record office scribe was, one may guess, a characteristic outlook shared by all the Bridge Clerks throughout the fifteenth century. Certainly, the surviving books of accounts they wrote imply that each of them enjoyed "employng his Wittes and diligence to the most availe and profaite of this place," for the quality of the writing remained consistently high. The evolution of Secretary Script and the mastery of English written forms in these records, moreover, offer circumstantial evidence that an awareness of Chancery practices on the part of the Bridge Clerks was a likely possibility. If in fact, as Fisher and others have argued, a precedent was set by Chancery clerks in developing writing standards during the last half of the fifteenth century, especially standards for writing English, that lead was soon followed in the Bridge House office. Eventually, it would also appear, that lead was overtaken.

LIST OF ABBREVIATIONS

BHA   *Bridge House Accounts*
BHD   *Ancient Deeds Among Bridge House Records*
BHE   *Expenditures of the Bridge*
CCR   *Calendar of the Close Rolls*
CPMR   *Calendar of Plea and Memoranda Rolls*
GL   Guildhall Library
JCCC   *Journals of the Court of Common Council*
LB   *Calendar of Letter-Books of the City of London*

NOTES

For permission to reproduce photographs of manuscripts in their keeping, I wish to thank The Scriveners' Company and The Guildhall Library, London, and The Huntington Library, San Marino, California.

1. Among government departments, it would appear that some were never very large, and yet each had requisite staff: the Privy Seal Office, for example, a keeper and five clerks and an equal number of assistants; the Great Wardrobe, a keeper and six clerical assistants, with additional clerks employed at various sites where the King's possessions

were stored (Orme 1973, 37). Within the judicial departments, however, much bigger staffs were called for. The Court of the King's Bench employed approximately fifteen senior officers and an equal number of assistants; the Court of Common Pleas, also about thirty officers and clerks; the Exchequer (even by the fourteenth century), twenty to thirty clerks serving the principal officers (Orme 1973, 37–38). In addition, Chancery, both in its Westminster court setting and in its record-keeping centers in or near Chancery Lane, employed at any given time about 120 clerks (many of them ordained clergy), including the twelve major clerks of the first form, the twelve clerks of the second form (all of whom had clerical assistants), and twenty-four cursitors (Fisher 1977, 877).

2. The earliest documentation of trade concentration in the area is found in the records of rentals of shops in Paternoster Row, the lane immediately to the north of the Cathedral churchyard, in a tenement owned by London Bridge. Between 1404 and c. 1410, seventeen tenants in these shops were members of the book trade: three stationers, three textwriters, four bookbinders, and seven limners. Within this group of book artisans were eight of the first known fourteen Wardens of the book-craft guild (Christianson 1987).

3. Among numerous examples, the following are illustrative: Peter Anketell, St. Bride, Fleet Street (GL 9171/3 (More), 469v); John Askewyth, St. Bride, Fleet Street (GL 9171/3 (More), 102v); Rowland Betot, St. Botolph without Aldersgate (GL 9171/2 (Brown), 26v); William Borden, St. Martin's Ludgate (GL 9171/3 (More), 460); Robert Bryan, St. Faith the Virgin (GL 9171/1 (Courtney), 259v); Thomas de Eydon, St. Sepulchre without Newgate (GL 9171/2 (Brown), 74); Thomas Plummer, St. Martin's Ludgate (GL 9171/5 (Sharp), 351v); Simon Skenne, St. Sepulchre without Newgate (GL 9171/2 (Brown), 280v); John Strech, St. Michael le Querne (GL 9171/1 (Courtney), 155).

4. Chaucer's associate, the mason Henry Yevele, for example, served as Warden at various times between 1368 and 1399. In the early fifteenth century, the post was occupied regularly by members of major guilds, such as the grocers William Chichele (1401), William Sevenoke (1404), William Wetenhale (1433–38); the mercer John Whatele (1404–18); the fishmonger Nicholas James (1418–20) (Welch 1894, 252–53; Thrupp 1948 [1962]).

5. Clerical staff included the Renter or collector of rents from tenants in the many Bridge properties; the Clerk of the Passage and the Drawbridge, who was responsible for Bridge tolls; and the Comptroller of

the Chamber and the Bridge (an office added late in the fifteenth century) (Welch 1894, 51). Also considered part of the Bridge staff was the Clerk of the Chapel of St. Thomas Becket, located on the Bridge. This clerk was assisted in his duties by a group of chaplains, usually four in number.
6. In the reign of Edward II, for example, a Guildhall clerk, John atte Hall, served as Renter (LB E, 52). In 1283, the clerk John de Claveringe was employed by the Wardens to collect alms and other gifts of endowment for the Bridge (BHD, C 36).
7. The exact dates for the tenures of John Parker and John Elys are not clearly indicated in the Bridge accounts, for expenditure records between 1446 and 1460 do not survive.
8. All Bridge records here noted are housed in the Corporation of London Records Office.
9. Photographs showing the writing of all the Bridge Clerks cited in this essay may be found in a series of plates accompanying Christianson 1987.
10. For discussion and illustration of earlier developments in the use of Secretary Script, see Parkes 1969 [1979].
11. Those signing declarations, in addition to Parker, as shown in Plate 2, are John Grove, Robert Bale, William Brampton, Thomas Clerk, Andrew Joye, William Olov, William Styfford, Thomas Froddesham, Robert Shodewell, Thomas Plumer, Robert Spayne, Richard Pumfrey, Peter Bonauntre, John Geton, Edward Noreys, and Henry Assheborn. Other scriveners, whose declarations appear on the following page (GL 5370, 16), are Walter Culpet and Thomas Tanner. With only slight variations, the declarations are formulaic (e.g., "I John Parker grannte [?graunte] and promitte to obserue the same to my power & subscribed with myn' onne [?oune] hande") and allow close comparisons of the hands to be made.
12. For discussion and examples of the features of Chancery Standard, see Fisher 1977, 883–85; Fisher, Richardson, and Fisher 1984, 26–51.
13. Examples of Normavyle's decorative penwork are found in BHA 1484–1509, 96, 119v–20. The first of these shows a bear motif, which, with only a slight reworking of its right paw, is an exact copy, but in reverse, of the figure of a bear appearing in the engraved "Nine Beasts of Prey," a playing card printed c. 1451–53, representing work by the Rhineland artist, the so-called Playing Card Master (Paris, Bibliothèque Nationale MS Kh 25 rés *Maître des cartes à jouer: Le Neuf des Animaux*).

For discussion of the dissemination of motifs on early playing cards, see van Buren and Edmunds 1974. For further discussion of Normavyle's decorative penwork, see Christianson 1987.

BIBLIOGRAPHY OF PRINCIPAL SOURCES

(i) In Manuscript

Cambridge, Trinity College
   R.3.2 (581).
London, Corporation of London Records Office
   Ancient Deeds Among Bridge House Records. 10 portfolios lettered A–K (saec. xii–xviii).
   Bridge House Accounts. Vols. 1–4 (1404–1509).
   Bridge House Estates Deeds: Large Register.
   Bridge House Estates Deeds: Small Register.
   Bridgemasters' Account Rolls. 17 rolls (1381–1405).
   Expenditures of the Bridge. Series 1 (1404–45).
   Journals of the Court of Common Council. Vols. 1–13 (1416–1536).
London, Guildhall Library
   5370 *Common Paper*.
   9171 *Register of Wills, Probate Acts, and Acts of Administration, Commissary Court, London*.
London, Lincoln's Inn
   Hale 187.
London, Sion College
   Arc. L 40.2/ E.44.
Paris, Bibliothèque Nationale
   Kh 25 rés *Maître des cartes à jouer*.
San Marino, California, The Huntington Library
   HM 39465.

(ii) Printed

Baker, J. H. "The English Legal Profession, 1450–1550." *Lawyers in Early Modern Europe and America*, edited by Wilfrid Prest, 16–41. New York: Holmes and Meier, 1981.
Burnley, J. D. "Curial Prose in England." *Speculum* 61 (1986):593–614.

Calendar of the Close Rolls Preserved in the Public Record Office. 61 vols. (1227–1509). London: H.M. Stationery Office, 1892–1963.

Chew, Helena M., ed. *London Possessory Assizes, A Calendar.* London: London Rec. Soc., 1965.

Christianson, C. Paul. "A Century of the Manuscript-Book Trade in Late Medieval London." *Medievalia et Humanistica* New Series 12 (1984):143–65.

―――. *A Directory of London Stationers and Book Artisans 1300–1500.* New York: Bibl. Soc. of America, forthcoming.

―――. "Early London Bookbinders and Parchmeners." *The Book Collector* 32 (1985):41–54.

―――. *Memorials of the Book Trade in Medieval London.* Woodbridge, Suffolk: Boydell and Brewer, 1987.

Courtenay, William J. "The London *Studia* in the Fourteenth Century." *Medievalia et Humanistica* New Series 13 (1985):127–41.

Crotch, W. J. B. *The Prologues and Epilogues of William Caxton. EETS* O.S. 176. London: Oxford University Press, 1928.

Doyle, A. I. and M. B. Parkes. "The production of copies of the *Canterbury Tales* and the *Confessio Amantis* in the early fifteenth century." *Medieval Scribes, Manuscripts and Libraries: Essays Presented to N.R. Ker,* edited by M. B. Parkes and Andrew G. Watson, 163–210. London: Scolar Press, 1978.

Fisher, John H. "Chancery and the Emergence of Standard Written English in the Fifteenth Century." *Speculum* 52 (1977):870–99.

Fisher, John H., Malcolm Richardson, and Jane L. Fisher. *An Anthology of Chancery English.* Knoxville: University of Tennessee Press, 1984.

Hastings, Margaret. *The Court of Common Pleas in Fifteenth Century England.* Ithaca: Cornell University Press, 1947; Hamden, Conn.: Shoe String Press, 1971.

Jones, P. E. "Some Bridge House Properties." *Jour. British Arch. Assoc.* Third Series 16 (1953):59–73.

Ker, N. R. *Medieval Manuscripts in British Libraries.* Vol. 1, *London.* Oxford: Clarendon Press, 1969.

Masters, Betty R. "The Records of the Bridge House Estates." *To God and the Bridge.* London: Guildhall Art Gallery Exhibition Catalogue, 1972, n.p.

Orme, Nicholas. *English Schools in the Middle Ages.* London: Methuen, 1973.

Parkes, M. B. *English Cursive Book Hands 1250–1500.* Oxford: Oxford University Press, 1969; London: Scolar Press, 1979.

————. "Palaeographical Description and Commentary." *Troilus and Criseyde*: *A Facsimile of Corpus Christi College Cambridge MS 61*. Cambridge: D.S. Brewer, 1978, 1–13.

Pollard, Graham. "The Company of Stationers Before 1557." *The Library* Fourth Series 18 (1937):1–38.

Richardson, Malcolm. "Henry V, the English Chancery, and Chancery English." *Speculum* 55 (1980):726–50.

Sharpe, R. R. *Calendar of Letter-Books of the City of London*. 11 vols. (1275–1498). London: John C. Francis, 1889–1912.

Simpson, W. Sparrow. *Chapters in the History of Old S. Paul's*. London: Elliot Stock, 1881.

Steer, Francis W. *Scriveners' Company Common Paper 1357–1628*. London: London Rec. Soc., 1968.

Thomas, A. H. and P. E. Jones, eds. *Calendar of Plea and Memoranda Rolls*. 6 vols. (1323–1482). Cambridge: Cambridge University Press, 1926–61.

Thrupp, Sylvia L. *The Merchant Class of Medieval London 1300–1500*. Ann Arbor: University of Michigan Press, 1948; 1962.

Unwin, George. *The Gilds and Companies of London*. 2nd ed. London: Methuen, 1908; 1925.

van Buren, Anne H. and Sheila Edmunds. "Playing Cards and Manuscripts: Some Widely Disseminated Fifteenth-Century Model Sheets." *The Art Bulletin* 56 (1974):12–30.

Welch, Charles. *History of the Tower Bridge, and of other bridges over the Thames built by the Corporation of London*. London: Smith, Elder, 1894.

Williams, Gwyn A. *Medieval London: From Commune to Capital*. London: Athlone, 1963.

The Standardization
of English Relative Clauses

Michael Montgomery

Nearly every year at least one student in a typical history of the English language class asks why it is that the Lord's Prayer in the King James Bible begins, "Our Father, *which* art in heaven." This question calls for a quick explanation of how *which* and other relative pronouns have developed in the history of the language—not an entirely easy task, since relative pronouns and other aspects of relative clauses have historically been as variable as any part of English. Since early Middle English, it is hardly possible to speak of categorical or near categorical patterning of aspects of relative clauses—the choice of pronoun used, the punctuation used, the types of antecedent nouns occurring with certain pronouns, the distance a relative clause may be separated from its antecedent noun, and so on. How then do we compare relative clauses in Modern English with Early Modern English, or with Middle English? How do we describe how relative clauses have changed over the past centuries? To what extent and at what point did—or have —they become standardized during the past six hundred years like many other linguistic patterns? These are the methodological and substantive questions addressed in this essay.

Most statements about the evolution of English relative clauses have been couched in general nonquantitative terms. Traugott (1972:152) provides a typical summary: "the diversity of relative clause patterns in ME [Middle English] and especially [Early Modern English] suggests there was considerable freedom in the use of relative clauses and extensive generalization of previously more limited forms. This generalization was later reversed and during [Modern English] constraints were reimposed to allow much less flexibility than was available" in Middle English and

Early Modern English. While valid as far as it goes, this kind of statement cannot be used in making comparisons between different periods and different varieties of English necessary to answer our questions above.

With few exceptions, the historical literature on English relative clauses offers similarly broad statements. Three studies that present quantitative findings can be cited. Quirk 1957 is a landmark study of relative clauses of educated twentieth-century British English, based on three groups of tape recordings and analyzing thirteen hundred examples. Many of its findings, such as those concerning the frequency of zero relative pronouns, are more characteristic of speech and thus are not relevant to our study of written relative clauses, but Quirk analyzes his data in terms of several of the linguistic factors we investigate, making further studies of spoken English easily comparable to his. Emma (1964:56–64) describes in detail Milton's use of relative pronouns, but the only quantitative figures he presents are percentage comparisons for Milton, as well as for Spenser and Donne, for the overall occurrence of different pronouns and their occurrence with personal and impersonal antecedents. His figures are consistent with the data analyzed here, in that the patterns they reveal are intermediate between those from our sixteenth-century and eighteenth-century texts.

The most intricate study of relative clauses in a written variety of English is Romaine's work on relativization in Middle Scots (1982). Both descriptive and theoretical, this study investigates the relationship between restrictives and nonrestrictives, the derivation of relative clauses from underlying structures, whether relativization with *that* and with *wh-* forms (*which, whom, who,* etc.) are derived in the same way, and what changes have taken place in the relative clause system from Middle Scots to modern Scots. Romaine displays the richness of her quantitative analysis in a series of tables (140 ff.), but because she deals with a variety of northern British English, a variety whose inventory of relative pronouns differs from the data we are concerned with here, it is beyond our scope to compare our findings to hers.

However, on the whole the literature has a crucial shortcoming: the lack of quantified statements that enable comparisons across sets of data. Admittedly, comparative studies are method-ologically difficult to design and carry out—requiring a researcher to control numerous variables such as type of text, mode of language, subject matter, author, style, among many others—but they are clearly necessary to approach definitive answers to the questions posed above.

The goals of this paper are 1) to discover what kinds of quantitative statements can be made about relative clauses at different stages of English, and specifically 2) to determine whether, how, and when English relative clause patterns became standardized. We will view standardization as the reduction of variation in the language and an increasing correspondence between linguistic form and linguistic function. The term thus does not refer to the achievement of national or standard status by a social or regional variety of the language such as London English. As used, the term is equivalent to 'regularization.' Relative pronouns and other features of relative clauses promise to be an especially fruitful and rich area in which to investigate the standardization of English, for at least two reasons:

1) The set of relative pronouns in Middle English was considerably larger and the choices more fluid than in Old English, when the general relative pronoun *þe* was well-nigh unconditional. From the twelfth century onward, the uninflected demonstrative pronoun *that* or *þat* came to be used for both singular and plural and was "the relative pronoun *par excellence* in Middle English" (Mossé 1952:62). Relative pronouns *which*, *who*, and *whom* all developed in Middle English, extending their original functions from interrogative to indefinite to simple relative (amply illustrated in Abbott 1888 and in the Oxford English Dictionary). The *OED* indicates that *which* was first used as a relative pronoun in 1175, *who* in 1297, and *whom* also in 1175. With each of these (and other) pronouns evolving independently and most likely at different rates, we should expect to find functional overlapping between them, in other words, considerable variation since the fourteenth century. To the extent that they have standardized since that time, we should expect to find fewer pronouns, more consistent use of pronouns, and more restrictions on pronouns in subsequent centuries.

2) Since Old English times, relative clauses in writing have sometimes been accompanied by punctuation. As the written language became standardized in the Early Modern English period, we would expect the punctuation of relative clauses to become less varied and more regular as well.

In supporting broad published statements like Traugott's cited above, some of our findings will not be surprising, but they are made here in a reliable way. The data in our analysis provide a baseline that enables us to consider a range of interesting research questions about the linguistic system governing the selection of relative pronouns and other relative clause features—not only historical questions about the standardization of the written language but also synchronic questions about differences in register between religious and nonreligious discourse. In the present study, we examine the precise occurrence of specific features of relative clauses in a large, unified body of material in order to trace the development of relative clauses and to throw clearer light on "standardization," which, as we will see, is not the one process of unidirectional, uniform reduction of variation that it is sometimes assumed to be. Rather, standardization, particularly for relative clauses, is more appropriately seen as a dynamic combination of processes involving many ongoing, interacting changes. In other words, different aspects of relative clauses were standardized at different times and at different rates, and while variation has greatly decreased over the centuries, much of it certainly remains.

DATA AND METHODOLOGY USED

To determine the time and manner in which relative clauses in English became standardized, it seems judicious to compare texts coming from different periods that are otherwise as identical as possible. Consequently, the data for the current study derive from four closely comparable written sources: four versions of one text, a book of the New Testament, the Acts of the Apostles. Each relative clause, more than sixteen hundred in all, has been culled from the four texts, which are distinguished chiefly by the different time periods whose language they represent, from the fourteenth to the twentieth century. This paper adopts a somewhat narrower definition of "relative clause" than has sometimes been used in the literature. The term is defined as a postnominal clause with a finite verb and a relative pronoun (such as *that* or *which*) that relates the clause to a "headnoun." Excluded are so-called "infinitival relative clauses" (as "a place *in which* to live") and "headless relative clauses" (as "*Where I live* is on Maple Street").

To permit their analysis, each of the 1,604 relative clauses in the four texts was coded according to a system of ten groups of formal and functional factors. These factors were: 1) type of relative clause (restrictive, nonrestrictive, or sentential); 2) relative pronoun used; 3) function of the relative pronoun in the relative clause; 4) function of the headnoun in the higher clause; 5) humanness or nonhumanness of the headnoun; 6) definiteness or indefiniteness of the headnoun; 7) presence and type of intervening material between the headnoun and the relative pronoun; 8) type of headnoun (common noun, proper noun, indefinite pronoun, etc.); 9) type of punctuation, if any, used with the relative clause; and 10) number of words between the headnoun and the relative pronoun. Using this coding system, a string of ten factors was assigned to each relative clause. We will focus primarily on the interaction of the choice of relative clause with other factors, particularly factors 1, 5, 7, 9, and 10.[*]

The four versions of Acts analyzed in this paper are as follows: 1) John Purvey's revision (c. 1390) of the John Wycliffe translation of Jerome's *Vulgate*. This text is written in a regional Middle English "standard literary language based on the dialects of the Central Midland counties, especially Northamptonshire, Huntingdonshire, and Bedfordshire" (Samuels 1969:407). It represents in its variety of word formation and spelling a text considered here typical of fourteenth-century English. This translation antedates the standardizing forces on the language—the printing press, the rising prestige of the London dialect, the influence of the Chancery style (Fisher, Richardson, and Fisher 1984), and others—that are usually cited as beginning in the fifteenth century. The original Wycliffe version (c. 1380) is not used in this study because it was a word-for-word, often awkward translation of Jerome's Latin and its phrasing was not representative of the English of the period.

2) The King James, or Authorized Version, first published in 1611, represents a sample of Early Modern English. Since its wording owes much to William Tyndale's translation of 1525 (Butterworth 1941:233) and its translators were conservative in phrasing and grammar, its language is considered here to be typical of the first half of the sixteenth century.

3) Rodolphus Dickinson's *A New and Corrected Version of the New Testament* was published in 1833, but its style "belongs more to the eighteenth century" (Pope 1952:543) and its language will be treated here as typical of that century. The authority of the Authorized Version was such that a new translation was not undertaken for 270 years. Dickinson's version, one of many revisions of the Authorized Version produced for "private reading," was motivated mainly by the obsolescence of King James English: "The lapse of centuries has produced a revolution in the English language, requiring a correspondent change in the version of the scriptures: and I may add, that the errors in grammar and rhetoric, the harsh and indelicate expressions, dispersed through the generally adopted text, demand amendment" (Dickinson 1833:vii).

4) Representing Late Modern English is the New English Bible translation, a collaborative product of Protestant churches in the United Kingdom. The NEB New Testament required thirteen years to translate and was first published in 1961. The data from this version are considered in this paper to be typical twentieth-century written English.

These four texts are thus identical in content, in authorship, and in most other important considerations; they enable us to undertake a comparison in which nearly all variables are controlled, all except the relatively minor ones discussed below:

1) One way our texts differ is that they are translations from different original documents, the Wycliffe being a translation from St. Jerome's Latin version, the King James Version and the New

English Bible being translations from nearly identical Greek texts, and Dickinson's edition a modernization of the King James language produced without consulting ancient texts.

2) Another way our texts differ is in the personal idiosyncrasies of the translators/revisers. There is no obvious method to assess any effect of these on the language, but it seems reasonable that the quantity of data we are examining from each version minimizes the possibility of this problem.

3) In addition, the translators/revisers of our four texts may have had different ideas about the most appropriate style for a religious text. Religious language is traditionally a conservative register; the force of this tradition has no doubt weakened in the past six centuries, but how? The King James translators deliberately strove for a formal, conservative style appropriate for public reading of Scripture, scrupulously using such markers of this style as the *-est* and *-eth* endings on second- and third-person singular verbs and not using the neuter possessive pronoun *its* that entered the language in the late sixteenth century. We indicated earlier that the language of Dickinson's version is also somewhat archaic for its publication date (1833). More than likely, a close comparison of both the Wycliffe and the New English Bible translations with contemporary nonreligious documents would show their styles have similar tendencies.

While these three factors might appear to differentiate the four texts in possibly significant ways and to present obstacles to their direct comparison, this is unlikely for several reasons. First, the ancient documents on which they were based, especially the King James and New English translations, were almost identical. Second, there is little reason to believe that the individual translations/ revisions used idiosyncratic phrasing, given that the King James and the New English translations were products of committee work, Purvey's revision was most likely carried out in consultation with others, and all four versions were efforts to use language familiar to the general public; in any case, the sets of data in this analysis are large enough to minimize any editorial idiosyncrasies. Third, it is unlikely that features of relative clauses (with the possible exception of *which* used with human and divine head-

Table 1. Type of Relative Clauses

	Wycliffe		King James		Dickinson		New English	
	n	%	n	%	n	%	n	%
Restrictive	231	58	232	53	223	53	247	71
Nonrestrictive	164	42	198	45	197	47	99	29
Sentential	1	0	10	2	2	0	0	0
Total	396	100	440	100	422	100	346	100

nouns) are as salient as many other grammatical features such as second-person pronouns and verb endings, and they are therefore unlikely to be excessively affected by the archaizing of style.

It might be suggested that a fourth variable mitigates the design of our study comparing texts from four periods over the past six hundred years of English: the specific set of antecedent nouns (called "headnouns" henceforth) that are modified by relative clauses is different for each text. In other words, the translators/revisers of the four texts chose to subordinate different clauses. The King James text has more relative clauses (440) than the others, nearly 100 more than the New English Bible; there are 246 relative clauses with human headnouns in the King James Version but only 158 in the New English Bible. Of the first 50 headnouns taking relative clauses in the King James text, for example, 2 do not correspond to headnouns in Wycliffe, 6 do not correspond to headnouns in Dickinson, and 13 do not do so in the New English Bible. What is translated in one version as a relative clause may be translated as a prepositional phrase, a participle, an adverbial clause, or another type of structure elsewhere.

While this discrepancy might make us wary that our texts are less comparable than we would like, there is good evidence that it reflects a difference in frequency of relative clauses and little else. In some respects, English relative clauses are remarkably consistent in our four texts, indicating that in some ways the relative clause system has changed little in six centuries. For instance, the ratio of restrictive to nonrestrictive clauses, as we see in Table 1,

Table 2. Type of Relative Clause for Different Functions of Relative Pronouns (R = Restrictive; N = Nonrestrictive)

	Wycliffe		King James		Dickinson		New English	
	R	N	R	N	R	N	R	N
Subject	67%	33%	64%	36%	62%	38%	69%	31%
Direct Object	46%	54%	44%	55%	47%	53%	79%	21%
Object of Preposition	33%	67%	31%	59%	30%	65%	65%	35%

Table 3. Type of Relative Clause for Different Functions of Headnoun

	Wycliffe	King James	Dickinson	New English
Subject	102	95	90	75
Direct Object	74	100	96	89
Object of Preposition	130	141	143	108
Object of Locative Prep.	22	22	20	27
Predicate Nominative	20	20	21	22
Object of Infinitive or Gerund	18	24	27	2
Other Functions	30	38	25	23

was similar until the twentieth century, but more significantly, the ratio of restrictives to nonrestrictives when the relative pronoun functioned as either subject, direct object, or object of preposition, as we see in Table 2, was even more consistent until the present century.

Our data also show great consistency over six hundred years in the different syntactic functions of the headnouns, as shown in Table 3. In other words, relative clauses have long been distributed in sentences in a similar fashion—always most often after objects of prepositions and much more often after main verbs of sentences than before them. Whatever changes have occurred in relative clauses—in relative pronouns, in punctuation used, etc.—the system in at least these three ways has shown stability.

*Table 4. Relative Pronouns Used**

	Wycliffe		King James		Dickinson		New English	
	R	N	R	N	R	N	R	N
Number of Different Pronouns Used	9		11		11		7	
Who	0	0	2	35	111	74	100	47
Whom	2	24	9	40	10	35	19	16
Preposition + Whom	1	16	3	9	4	12	0	0
Whose	1	6	2	11	4	16	5	5
That	187	42	104	0	18	0	52	0
Which	15	52	97	81	56	41	35	19
Preposition + Which	23	18	1	1	12	11	0	0
The + Which	0	0	0	4	0	1	0	0
Whichever	1	0	0	0	0	0	0	0
Where	1	4	5	8	6	7	10	12
Where + Preposition**	0	2	6	8	0	0	0	0
Wherefore	0	0	3	1	0	0	0	0
Why	0	0	0	0	1	0	0	0
When	0	0	0	0	1	0	0	0
Nothing	0	0	0	0	0	0	26	0
Total	231	164	232	198	223	197	247	99

*Excludes sentential relative clauses
**E.g., *whereby*, *wherein*

TYPES OF RELATIVE CLAUSES AND PRONOUNS

As we proceed with our analysis, we will first take an overview of our data. Then we will examine the four main relative pronouns that occur—*that, which, who,* and *whom*—to determine how their functions have developed since the fourteenth century. After this, we will consider the proximity of relative clauses to their head-nouns and finally the punctuation used in relative clauses. We will then offer some concluding remarks about the standardization of relative clause patterns since Middle English.

Table I shows the types of relative clauses—restrictive, non-restrictive, and sentential—in the four sets of data. Table 4 presents the different relative pronouns used from the fourteenth to the twentieth century. (Because of their infrequency, sentential relative clauses, which modify an entire clause rather than a single headnoun, like *God has raised up this Jesus, of which we all are witnesses* from Dickinson's version, will not be discussed in this paper; in some tables, as in 5 and 7 below, discrepancies in subtotals are due to the counting of sentential relatives for some of the ten factors and not for others.)

GENERAL OBSERVATIONS

Restrictive relative clauses occur with almost equal frequency in all four sets of data, but the situation differs for nonrestrictives, which occur only half as often in the twentieth-century data as in the eighteenth or sixteenth century. This may reflect a stylistic choice by NEB translators to render structures from Greek differently from the King James version. It may also reflect the adoption of a tighter, more direct, and less formal style with fewer appositional elements; further evidence supporting this from Table 4 is the lack of formal-sounding preposition + relative clause collocations (*to whom, from which*, etc.) in the NEB and the use of the zero relative pronoun (as in *the great things Ø God has done*) only in the NEB.

We also observe that relative pronouns were standardized in neither Middle English (when *who* had yet to occur) nor Early Modern English. The greatest variety of pronouns, if we count compound relatives like *wherein* and *whereto* separately, occurred in the sixteenth century. By the eighteenth century, the major relative pronouns had more or less acquired their modern-day restrictions and had approached standardization, although the range of pronouns was much greater and much more variation in usage still existed than in the twentieth century.

FOUR RELATIVE PRONOUNS

In this section we examine in turn the development of the four most common relative pronouns in our data—*that, which, whom,* and *who*—particularly with respect to their use in different types of relative clauses and with different types of headnouns, relying on Tables 4–10. For reasons of space, we ignore comparisons of other relative pronouns, like *whose, where,* and others, although these might give us interesting sidelights on the process of standardization. In this discussion, we incorporate the data on divine headnouns with that on human headnouns under the latter designation; preliminary analysis indicates that relative pronouns pattern the same with both. We will now examine more closely each of these four pronouns.

That / That was the most common relative pronoun in Middle English. From Table 4 we see it was used with 187/231 (81%) of the restrictives (as in sentence 1) and with more than one-quarter of the nonrestrictive clauses (in sentences 2 and 3 below) in the Wycliffe version.

1) of all the thingis, *that* Jhesus bigan for to do and teche. (Wycliffe, Acts 1:2)
2) And thei ordeyneden tweyne, Joseph, *that* was clepid Barsabas, . . . (Wycliffe, Acts 1:22)
3) And thei preieden, and seiden, Thou, Lord, that knowist the hertis of alle men. (Wycliffe, Acts 1:24)

That became restricted to one type of clause early, by the sixteenth century occurring only with restrictives, its modern-day use, and is the only pronoun to have been so limited (Table 4). Accounting for its frequency in Middle English, and to a lesser extent in Early Modern English, is its common occurrence with both human and divine headnouns (seen in sentences 2 and 3 above, sentence 4 below; cf. Table 5), a use that has almost entirely disappeared in Modern English except with a pronominal headnoun (sentence 5). In Middle English, *that* was used 82 times with nonhuman headnouns, a practice that, curiously, disappeared almost completely in Early Modern English (only 4 instances) before being reestablished in Modern English as the general tendency (Table 6).

4) For the promise is unto you, and to your children, and to all *that* are afar off. (KJV, Acts 2:39)
5) And they declared to him the word of the Lord, and to all *that* were in his house. (Dickinson, Acts 16:32)

In summary, we can see that *that* evolved from its predominant position as the most common relative pronoun in fourteenth-century English to a more limited status in more recent times; it had gained its modern-day constraints of use in restrictive clauses with nonhuman headnouns by the eighteenth century (Tables 7–11). Even so, the data suggest that since Middle English, *which* has competed with and has partially replaced *that* in restrictive clauses with nonhuman headnouns, at least in formal, written style.

Which / The second most prevalent relative pronoun in Middle English is *which*, which occurred 108 times (Table 4). Like *that*, *which* had diverse functions in the fourteenth century—in both restrictives (sentences 6 and 7) and nonrestrictives (sentences 8 and 9), and with both human (sentence 8) and nonhuman headnouns (sentence 6), as we see from Tables 4–6.

6) This is the stoon, which was repreued of you bildinge, . . . (Wycliffe, Acts 4:11)
7) it is not youre for to have knowe tymes or momentis, *whiche* the fadir hath put in his power; (Wycliffe, Acts 1:7)
8) abide the biheest of the fadir, which ye herden (Wycliffe, Acts 1:4)
9) to the irun gate that leedith to the citee, *which* wilfully is opened to hem. (Wycliffe, Acts 12:10)

This diversity continued into Early Modern English, when *which* became the most common pronoun overall, occurring 106 times with human and divine headnouns (Table 5), and 77 times with nonhuman headnouns (Table 6). Its chief differences from *that* in these periods are two: the greatly decreased use of *that* with nonhuman headnouns in the sixteenth century (a tendency not reversed, and then only in part, until the twentieth century, see Table 6), and the tendency of *which* to occur in relative clauses separated from their headnouns by other structures (like a prepositional phrase, in sentence 10, or another relative clause, in sentence 11) and thus be more loosely integrated into the sentence.

10) until the time of the restitution of all things, *which* God hath spoken by the mouth of all. (KJV, Acts 3:21)
11) This is the stone that was set at nought of you builders, *which* is become the head of the corner. (KJV, Acts 4:11)

More than one-half of the relative clauses (53.7%) with *which* in Middle English, and more than one-quarter of them (27%) in Early Modern English, have intervening material between the headnoun and *which* (Tables 7 and 8). We will focus on this point in detail in a later section, but in summary, we see that the relative pronoun *which*, like *that*, had substantially gained its modern-day use with nonhuman headnouns and in both restrictive and nonrestrictive clauses by the eighteenth century.

Whom / Like *which*, *whom* began to be used as a relative pronoun in the twelfth century and occurred predominantly in nonrestrictive clauses in Middle English (Table 4). Examples of early nonrestrictive uses of *whom* are sentences 12 and 13.

12) Jhesu of Nazareth, a man prouyd of God in you by vertues, or myracles, and wondris, and tokenes, the whiche God dide by him in the myddel of you, . . . *Whom* God reyside, the sorwis of helle vnboundun, vp that it was inpossible him for to be holdyn of it. (Wycliffe, Acts 2:22–23)
13) for God reyside and hym the Lord and Crist, this Jhesu, *whom* ye crucifieden. (Wycliffe, Acts 2:36)

Unlike *which*, *whom* did not become as common in restrictives as in nonrestrictives until much later—the twentieth century (Table 4)—and its use with nonhuman headnouns has never been more than marginal (see Table 6), with the two instances of this in our data given below:

Table 5. Pronouns used with Human and Divine Headnouns

	Wycliffe	KJV	Dickinson	NEB
That	147	100	4	1
Which	58	106	12	4
Who	0	37	185	147
Whom	40	61	61	34
Total	245	304	262	186

Table 6. Pronouns used with Nonhuman Headnouns

	Wycliffe	KJV	Dickinson	NEB
That	82	4	14	51
Which	52	77	109	50
Who	0	0	0	0
Whom	1	0	0	1
Total	135	81	123	102

14) And unnethe we bi sydis seylinge, camen into sum place, that is clepid of good hauene, to *whom* the citee Tessala was nyg. (Wycliffe, Acts 27:8)

15) possessed the nations *whom* God drove out before them. (NEB, Acts 7:45)

Whom has been the slowest to develop an attachment to its headnouns, so to speak, with more than half the relative clauses in both Middle English (53.5%) and Early Modern English (52.5%), and nearly half of them in the eighteenth century (45.4%), occurring with material between the headnoun and the clause (Tables 7–9).

Who / The relative pronoun which has evolved more than any other since Middle English is *who*. Of the four pronouns considered in detail, it is the latecomer, never occurring in the

Table 7. Comparison of Relative Pronouns in Fourteenth-Century English

	That	Which*	Who	Whom*
With Human Headnoun	130	50	0	17
With Divine Headnoun	17	6	0	22
With Nonhuman Headnoun	82	52	0	4
With No Headnoun	0	1	0	0
Without Intervening Material	200	50	0	20
With Intervening Material:	29	58	0	23
1–4 Words	26	24	0	6
5–8 Words	2	17	0	9
9 or More Words	1	17	0	8
% with Intervening Material	12.7	53.7	0	53.5
Total	229	109	0	43

*Includes use with preposition

Wycliffe translation (Tables 4, 7). In Early Modern English, it occurred 37 times, barely half as often as *whom*, and only one-third as regularly as *which* with human or divine headnouns (Tables 4, 8); herein lies the answer to the student's query at the first of the paper. By the eighteenth century, *who* had become the most common pronoun with human headnouns and the most frequent overall, reflecting its modern-day function, and reflecting the prominent role of human and divine individuals in the narrative text of Acts (Table 5). In this regard, *who* replaced *that* and *which*, the dominant pronouns in the fourteenth and sixteenth centuries (Table 5). Perhaps most striking about *who* is its later development than *whom*, which is revealed not only in our data but also in the Fisher et al. anthology of fifteenth-century Chancery English documents, in which *who* occurs only twice as a relative pronoun, as compared to the much more frequent *whom* (1984:45). In several respects, however, as in the percentage of relative clauses with *who* that have intervening material between relative pronoun and headnoun, *who* had by the eighteenth century overtaken *whom* in acquiring its modern-day patterns of usage (Tables 7–9).

Table 8. *Comparison of Relative Pronouns in Sixteenth-Century English*

	That	*Which**	*Who*	*Whom**
With Human Headnoun	70	93	32	39
With Divine Headnoun	30	13	5	21
With Nonhuman Headnoun	4	77	0	1
With No Headnoun	0	2	0	0
Without Intervening Material	98	135	13	29
With Intervening Material:	6	50	24	32
1–4 Words	5	31	5	10
5–8 Words	0	12	5	9
9 or More Words	1	7	14	13
% with Intervening Material	5.8	27.0	64.9	52.5
Total	104	185	37	61

*Includes use with preposition

Table 9. *Comparison of Relative Pronouns in Eighteenth-Century English*

	That	*Which**	*Who*	*Whom**
With Human Headnoun	4	12	164	35
With Divine Headnoun	0	0	21	25
With Nonhuman Headnoun	14	109	0	1
With No Headnoun	0	2	0	0
Without Intervening Material	17	99	139	33
With Intervening Material:	1	22	46	28
1–4 Words	0	14	20	9
5–8 Words	0	6	10	6
9 or More Words	1	2	16	13
% with Intervening Material	5.6	18.2	24.9	45.4
Total	18	123	185	61

*Includes use with preposition

Table 10. Comparison of Relative Pronouns in Twentieth-Century
English

	That	Which*	Who	Whom*
With Human Headnoun	1	3	126	18
With Divine Headnoun	0	1	20	15
With Nonhuman Headnoun	51	50	1	2
Without Intervening Material	47	40	125	28
With Intervening Material:	5	14	22	7
1–4 Words	2	11	17	1
5–8 Words	2	3	4	1
9 or More Words	1	0	1	0
% with Intervening Material	9.6	25.9	15.0	20.0
Total	52	54	147	35

*Includes use with preposition

PROXIMITY OF RELATIVE CLAUSE
TO HEADNOUN

It was suggested above that a significant difference between *that*
and *which* in Middle and Early Modern English was that the latter
was frequently removed from its headnoun. Examples of this are
in sentence 8 above, where a prepositional phrase interposes between the relative clause and its headnoun, and in sentence 9,
where a relative clause does the same thing. In this regard, *which*
resembles the other *wh-* pronouns, *whom* and *who*. Tables 7–
10 indicate the frequency of lengths of material, in numbers of
words, which separate each of the four major pronouns from their
headnouns, and Tables 11 and 12 below show the types of intervening structures that occur. In Middle English, the majority of
relative clauses with *which* or *whom*, and in Early Modern English the majority of clauses with *whom* or *who*, are separated
from the headnouns. On the other hand, *that* had evolved by Early
Modern English to being much more closely tied to its headnoun,
with only 6 of 104 cases in the sixteenth century not following
the headnoun directly. Sentences 16 and 17 show that the relative

Table 11. *Material Between Headnoun and Relative Pronoun*

	Wycliffe		King James		Dickinson		New English	
	R	N	R	N	R	N	R	N
No Material	209	73	210	96	204	111	220	74
Adverb Prepositional or Other Phrase	7	17	7	33	5	32	15	14
Appositive	0	15	2	15	2	11	1	6
Adjective	0	3	0	3	0	2	1	2
Verb Phrase	10	17	10	17	7	16	6	1
Relative Clause	0	22	2	17	4	15	3	1
One or More Intervening Clauses	5	10	0	6	0	5	0	0
Other	0	7	1	11	1	5	1	1
Total with Material	22	91	22	102	19	86	27	25
% with Intervening Material	28.6		28.8		25.0		15.0	
Total	231	164	232	198	223	197	247	99

clause may occur at a considerable distance from its headnoun (*man*, *Jesus Christ*).

16) And a certain man lame from his mother's womb was carried, *whom* they laid daily at the gate of the temple which is called Beautiful, to ask alms of them that entered into the temple; *Who*, seeing Peter and John about to go into the temple, asked an alms. (KJV, Acts 3:2–3)

17) And he shall send Jesus Christ, which before was preached unto you: *Whom* the heaven must receive until the times. (KJV, Acts 3:20–21)

Reflecting the extension from indefinite pronouns to relatives, such a use of *who* in 17 has a partially conjunctive sense equivalent to *and he* (Abbott 1888:179) and a rhetorical force as well, which allowed the clause to follow its headnoun at a considerable distance, even two to three clauses later. By the eighteenth cen-

Table 12. Number of Words between Headnoun and Relative Pronoun

	Wycliffe		King James		Dickinson		New English	
	R	N	R	N	R	N	R	N
Without Intervening Material	209	73	210	96	204	111	220	74
With Intervening Material:	22	91	22	102	19	86	27	25
1–4 Words	18	42	16	40	12	37	22	16
5–8 Words	3	24	4	26	2	21	4	7
9 or More Words	1	25	2	36	5	28	1	2
% with Intervening Material	9.5	55.5	9.5	51.5	8.5	43.6	10.9	25.3

tury, the percentage of nonrestrictive relative clauses with intervening material had fallen below one-half, to 43.6%, but even so, Table 12 indicates that 105 clauses (19 restrictives and 86 non-restrictives) were not adjacent to their headnouns. Only in the twentieth century does this percentage fall significantly.

A more revealing view of this comes from examining not the frequency of separated headnouns but the types and amounts of material intervening. Table 11 indicates that a variety of linguistic elements may appear between headnouns and relative pronouns, elements that we may classify as either minor or major. Adverbial prepositional phrases, other phrases, appositives, and postnominal adjectives are minor in the sense that they are usually short and are more tightly bound to a headnoun. In most cases, these elements, rather than the relative clause, must follow the headnoun immediately. Sentences 18–19 have prepositional phrases after the headnouns (*promise, men*), forcing the relative clause to follow:

18) but wait for the promise of the Father, *which*, saith he, ye have heard of me. (KJV, Acts 1:4)
19) There stood beside them two men in white *who* said, (NEB, Acts 1:10)

Table 13. Minor and Major Elements Intervening between Headnoun
and Relative Pronoun

	Wycliffe		King James		Dickinson		New English	
	R	N	R	N	R	N	R	N
Minor Elements	7	35	9	51	7	45	17	22
Major Elements	15	49	12	40	11	36	9	2
Other	0	7	1	11	1	5	1	1
Total with Material	22	91	22	102	19	86	27	25

Other structures—verb phrases, relative clauses, and other clauses —are major, involving larger and more prominent constituents. Sentences 20 and 21 have verb phrases after the headnouns (*men*, *thing*), which moves the relative clauses after the main clause.

20) Two men stood by them in white apparel; *which* also said. (KJV, Acts 1:10)

21) I had a vision: a thing was coming down *that* looked like a great sheet of sail-cloth. (NEB, Acts 11:4)

Table 13 collapses figures in Table 11 and compares the frequency of minor and major intervening structures across the four sets of data. The number of intervening minor elements has remained roughly equal since Middle English, except for the twentieth-century data, in which 15 restrictive relatives (Table 11) have a prepositional phrase intervening, as in sentence 20 above. Most striking is the decline of major elements from 64 in the fourteenth century to 11 in the twentieth century, particularly with nonrestrictive clauses (all of which involved *wh-* pronoun forms). The number of intervening clauses declined from 37 in Wycliffe to 4 in NEB, and the number of verb phrases from 23 to 7.

The pronouns *which*, *who*, and *whom*, as is evident from Tables 7–10, have evolved independently toward tighter integration with headnouns. *Which*, separated from its headnoun 53.7% of the time in Middle English, was separated only 27% of the time in Early Modern English, close to the twentieth-century figure (25.9%). *Whom* gradually became more integrated from the fourteenth to the eighteenth century (declining from 53.5% separation to 45.4%), before dropping significantly in the twentieth century to 20%. *Who*, not used in Middle English, dropped quickly from 64.9% separation in the sixteenth century to 24.9% two centuries later.

Thus, it appears from our data that either this aspect of written relative clauses—the relationship of a relative clause to its head-noun—is still evolving or it has become standardized for *which*, *who*, and *whom* only in the twentieth century.

PUNCTUATION USED WITH RELATIVE CLAUSES

With the advent of printing in the late fifteenth century and the development of mass publication in the next, punctuation became to readers a set of symbols for indicating the grammatical and rhetorical relationships of words, phrases, and clauses to one another. Table 14 shows the variety and frequency of punctuation used to set off relative clauses, and Table 15 shows the punctuation used with different relative pronouns in the four stages of English. Considerable variety in punctuation occurs in the sixteenth and eigh-

Table 14. Punctuation Used with Different Types of Relative Clauses

	Wycliffe		King James		Dickinson		New English	
	R	N	R	N	R	N	R	N
No Punctuation	163	6	213	4	161	13	236	2
Comma	67	120	16	130	57	133	11	96
Semicolon	0	17	1	17	2	37	0	0
Colon	0	0	2	33	1	12	0	0
Period	1	21	0	11	0	1	0	0
Parentheses	0	0	0	3	0	1	0	1
Dash	0	0	0	0	2	0	0	0
Total	231	164	232	198	223	197	247	99

Table 15. *Punctuation Used with Different Pronouns*

	That	Which	Who	Whom	Others
Wycliffe					
With no Punctuation	152	12	0	3	2
With Comma	76	72	0	29	11
With Semicolon	1	12	0	3	1
With Period	0	13	0	8	1
% with Punctuation	33.2	89.0	0	93.0	
King James					
With No Punctuation	99	95	1	9	13
With Comma	5	74	14	29	
With Semicolon	0	4	0	9	6
With Colon	0	9	14	11	3
With Parentheses	0	2	4	4	6
With Period	0	2	1	0	0
% with Punctuation	4.9	48.6	97.3	85.2	
Dickinson					
With No Punctuation	14	57	87	5	4
With Comma	4	55	74	36	22
With Semicolon	0	5	19	14	1
With Colon	0	5	2	6	1
% with Punctuation	22.2	53.7	53.0	91.8	
New English					
With no Punctuation	50	33	97	18	40
With Comma	2	21	49	17	18
% with Punctuation	3.8	38.9	34.0	48.6	

teenth century, with a number of marks being used—semicolons, colons, periods, parentheses, and dashes—that no longer occur with relative clauses. The most dramatic development in punctuation comes between Dickinson and the New English Bible, with standardization to the modern-day pattern—no punctuation with restrictives and a comma with nonrestrictives—only in the twentieth century. Although the New English Bible data indicate that 11 / 107 (10.3%) of the commas occur with restrictive clauses, as in sentence 22, nearly all of these have an intervening nonrestrictive appositive which accounts for the comma.

22) There were seven sons of Sceva, a Jewish chief priest, who were using this method. (NEB, Acts 19:14)

STANDARDIZATION

In this paper we have examined several facets of the development of relative clauses in English, relying on four sizable corpora of data to permit us to outline prominent trends in this complex area of the language. Our analysis not only suggests the rich possibilities of studying subsystems of a language like relativization in order to describe the evolving structure of English, but it allows us to address the question of standardization raised at the beginning of this paper. If we understand standardization to refer to the reduction of variation in language and the achievement of a relatively simple formal-functional correspondence, then we can make the following summary statements about the standardizing of relative clauses in written English:

1) Relative pronouns became standardized in a different order (*that* > *which* > *who* > *whom*) from the one in which they entered the language (*that* > *which* > *whom* > *who*), indicating that each pronoun became standardized at its own pace and that each has its own history.

2) *That* was the first relative pronoun to become functionally specialized, becoming confined to restrictive clauses. However, since Early Modern English, the ancient supremacy of *that* as a relative pronoun has declined, at least in written English, and there has been an increasing tendency for *wh-* forms, especially *who* and *whom*, to replace *that* with human headnouns and for *wh-* relative pronouns to replace *that* in restrictive clauses.

3) Relative pronouns had become standardized for the type of headnouns they took—*that* and *which* with nonhumans, *who* and *whom* with humans—by the eighteenth century.

4) There has been a continuing tendency since Middle English

to reduce the degree of separation of a relative clause from its headnoun, or to put it another way, an increasing tendency for nonrestrictive relative clauses to become more closely attached to their headnouns. It is unclear whether this has yet become standardized in modern-day written English.

5) Punctuation for relative clauses did not become standardized until the twentieth century.

6) Features of relative clauses in the sixteenth century were most variable, with much standardization taking place in the following two centuries, but a significant degree of variation remains in present-day patterns.

*The coding strings of each dataset were analyzed according to the VARBRUL 2 program designed by Susan Pintzuk of the University of Pennsylvania and David Sankoff of the University of Montreal, among others.

REFERENCES

Abbott, E. A. *A Shakespearian Grammar*. New York: London, 1888.
Butterworth, Charles C. *The Literary Lineage of the King James Bible 1340–1611*. Philadelphia: University of Pennsylvania Press, 1944.
Cammack, Melvin Macye. *John Wyclif and the English Bible*. New York: American Tract Society, 1938.
Dickinson, Rodolphus. *New and Corrected Version of the New Testament; or, a Minute Revision, and Professed Translation of the Original Histories, Memoirs, Letters, Prophecies, and Other Productions of the Evangelists and Apostles; to Which are Subjoined, a Few, Generally Brief, Critical, Explanatory, and Practical Notes*. Boston: Lilly, Wait, Colman, and Holden, 1833.
Emma, Ronald David. *Milton's Grammar*. The Hague: Mouton, 1964.
Fisher, John H., Malcolm Richardson, and Jane L. Fisher. *An Anthology of Chancery English*. Knoxville: University of Tennessee Press, 1984.
Forshall, Rev. Josiah, and Sir Frederic Madden, ed. *The Holy Bible, Containing the Old and New Testaments, with the Apochryphal Books in the Earliest English Versions made from the Latin Vulgate by John*

Wycliffe and his Followers. 4 volumes. Oxford: Oxford University Press, 1850.

Mitchell, Bruce. *Old English Syntax*. 2 volumes. New York: Oxford University Press, 1985.

Mosse, Fernand. *A Handbook of Middle English*. Baltimore, Md.: Johns Hopkins Press, 1952.

Pope, Hugh. *English Versions of the Bible*. Revised and amplified by Rev. Sebastian Bullough. St. Louis, Mo.: Herder, 1952.

Quirk, Randolph. "Relative Clauses in Educated Spoken English." *English Studies* 38 (1957), 97–107.

Romaine, Suzanne. *Socio-historical Linguistics: its Status and Methodology*. Cambridge: Cambridge University Press, 1982.

Samuels, M. L. "Some Applications of Middle English Dialectology." In *Approaches to English Historical Linguistics: An Anthology*, edited by Roger Lass, 404–18. New York: Holt, Rinehart and Winston, 1969.

Traugott, Elizabeth. *A History of English Syntax: a Transformational Approach to the History of English Sentence Structure*. New York: Holt, Rinehart and Winston, 1972.

Americanisms, Briticisms, and the Standard: An Essay at Definition

John Algeo

The discovery that the English language exists in a number of independent national standards has been gradually and, for some discoverers, reluctantly made. All of us tend, as a practical matter, to think of the variety of the language we use as "the" language and of other varieties as curious departures from the rational, simple, and esthetic norm represented by our own language habits. That is a human attitude.

That natural and inevitable habit of thought is reinforced in British speakers by the fact that the land in which they live is the site of the mother language from which all forms of worldwide English are derived. But present-day British English has no more claim to identity with that mother language—English of the sixteenth century and earlier—than do any other forms of English now spoken around the world.

In 1582, in *The First Part of the Elementarie*, Richard Mulcaster, who confessed "I honor the *Latin*, but I worship the *English*" (254), felt compelled to defend the use of his native language for learned purposes, acknowledging that "our English tung . . . is of small reatch, it stretcheth no further then this Iland of ours, naie not there ouer all" (256). Mulcaster could not have foreseen how quickly and how widely the "small reatch" of English was to be extended.

However, the generation after Mulcaster was to see the foundation of Jamestown in 1607 and of Plymouth Colony in 1620. Those events marked the beginning of the spread of English and led to an eventual diversification of the mother tongue and the evolution of separate national standards, first in Britain and the

United States and later, by a process that is still continuing, in Australia, Canada, the Caribbean, India, New Zealand, South Africa, and elsewhere.

In Mulcaster's day there was no British English because there was no non-British English with which to contrast it. Before 1607 there was only English. After 1776 there was British English, American English, and eventually a number of other such national varieties, each constituting its own standard—all ultimately derived from the same mother source and none having a greater claim to identity with that source. Geography is not tantamount to linguistic continuity.

The propensity of the English to identify the form of the language they speak with the English language per se is augmented by the fact that the term *English* is ambiguous. It refers either to the English language in all its varieties around the world or to one particular variety, that used in the southern part of the largest British island. The ambiguity is sometimes exploited by using the term *English English* for the latter referent, but that term is awkward at best.

The problem of terminology exemplified by *English* extends to the terms used for the major national standards of the language and their distinctive features. The suffix *-ism* has been specialized to denote (in the words of the *OED*) "a peculiarity or characteristic, esp. of language, e.g. Aeolism, Americanism, Anglicism, Atticism, Devonshirism, Gallicism, Graecism, Hebraism, Hellenism, Latinism, Orientalism, Scotticism, Southernism, Westernism, etc.," to which might be added such terms as *colloquialism*, *legalism*, and *malapropism*. Within that still broad sense of *-ism*, a more restricted use is to denote a feature belonging to a national standard of an international language, for English: *Americanism*, *Australianism*, *Briticism*, *Canadianism*, and *Hibernicism* or *Irishism*. Terms like *New-Zealandism* and *South-Africanism*, although logically parallel, are generally avoided, perhaps as awkward, and so do not appear in dictionaries.

Such terms, for which we may use the generic *nationalism*, apparently derive from Greek *Hellenismos* 'an expression in the proper Greek manner.' A number of the terms came to denote the imitation in one language of the manner of expression typical of another, as an *Anglicism* in French or a *Celticism, Gallicism, Hebraism*, or *Latinism* in English. However, the earliest Greek use of the suffix with application to language seems to have been in reference to a national or cultural standard.

Terms for national standards of English were late in developing. *Scotticism* was used as early as 1717 by DeFoe, but the *OED*'s definition of the term, "an idiom or mode of expression characteristic of Scots; esp. as used by a writer of English," regards it as a foreign importation into English, not as part of a national variant, and indeed by 1717 there was no Scottish national standard because there was no longer a Scottish nation. Nevertheless, that term was the model on which *Americanism*, the first of the nationalisms, was developed. The *OEDS* cites Witherspoon, writing in 1781: "The word Americanism, which I have coined for the purpose, is exactly similar in its formation and significance to the word Scotticism."

The use for which Witherspoon coined the term was, in his own words, as follows:

> Americanisms, by which I understand an use of phrases or terms, or a construction of sentences, even among persons of rank or education, different from the use of the same terms or phrases, or the construction of similar sentences, in Great Britain.

The earlier pejorative sense of *Scotticism* is still reflected in Witherspoon's apologetic "even among persons of rank or education." The confidence of the new nation in its own speechways as a standard had not yet reached the visionary level articulated by Noah Webster twenty-five years later in the 1806 preface to his dictionary: "In fifty years from this time, the American-English will be spoken by more people, than all the other dialects of the language."

It is certainly no accident that the first two terms for national variants of English, representing the first and still major national varieties, were both American inventions—*Americanism* by Witherspoon in 1781 and *Briticism* by Richard Grant White in 1868 (at least the earliest *OED* citation for the latter term is from

White). Other such terms tagged along—*Australianism* in 1891 and *Canadianism* in 1928. It was the sense of national identity, culture, and destiny in the United States that led Americans first to accept a national standard of English in their own country, distinct from that of England.

The acceptance of an American standard has implicit within it a recognition that the language of the quondam motherland is only another national variety, and not a universal standard for English. The fact that *Briticism* followed *Americanism* by nearly a hundred years testifies to the slowness with which such acceptance comes. Understandably, it is slower in more recently independent nations like New Zealand, though perhaps slowest of all in England itself.

Thomas Pyles told of a conversation he had in the 1950s with an English woman who responded to his use of the expression *British English* with a merry laugh and the objection, "Why, what other kind is there?" And Allen Walker Read encountered resistance from a distinguished British publisher to the proposed title "A Dictionary of Briticisms." Many of the English do not like the word *Briticism*. There is doubtless a complex of reasons for the distaste with which they regard the word, but one of the reasons is surely that the term challenges the flattering, but unexamined, assumption that the English language is whatever is used in England and nothing else.

The slowness to realize that English exists only in a variety of national standards is also evident in the lexicographical treatment, or lack of treatment, of terms from and denoting those national standards. Although most general dictionaries now make a conscientious effort to include all frequently used vocabulary, or as much of it as their users are likely to want, even *Webster's Third New International*—clearly the best of the synchronic dictionaries —is conspicuously weak on including and labeling terms from national varieties other than its own. On the whole, British dictionaries do a better job of entering and identifying Americanisms, Briticisms, and other nationalisms than do American books. For that superiority, there are historical, marketing, and cultural explanations in addition to whatever incidental devotion the editors may feel to a lexicographical ideal.

Some curious lacunae exist, however, in the lexicographical treatment of terms for nationalisms. An implicational scale could be constructed for the inclusion of nationalisms in dictionaries. Any dictionary that enters a term from the following list will also enter all terms above it on the list and no terms below it:

Americanism: *Collins Cobuild, Longman Dictionary of Contemporary English, Oxford Advanced Learner's*
Briticism: *Funk & Wagnalls New Standard, Oxford Reference, Webster's Ninth New Collegiate*
Australianism: *Chambers 20th Century, Concise Oxford, Longman Dictionary of the English Language, Reader's Digest Great Illustrated*
Canadianism: *Collins Dictionary of the English Language, Oxford English Dictionary* plus *Supplement, Webster's Third*

This scale may reflect the frequency of the terms and the inclusiveness of the dictionaries, but it also reflects how well and how long the nationalisms have been established.

The three books that enter only *Americanism* are "learner's" dictionaries of the advanced sort—works, as it happens by British publishers, for mature students of English as a foreign language. The implication that might be drawn from the editorial decision to enter *Americanism* but not *Briticism* is that Americanisms are departures from a norm of British English assumed by the dictionary. Similarly, *The Oxford Reference Dictionary* enters *American English*, but not *British English*, with the same implication. Such a decision, whatever other explanation may be offered for it, invites an ethnocentric bias on the part of the dictionary user.

When terms for nationalisms are entered in dictionaries, their definitions are also noteworthy. They can be exemplified by seventy entries distributed among nineteen dictionaries, with emphasis on British works, since they are generally superior in attending to the referents of those terms:

Chambers 20th Century Dictionary, new ed., 1983.
Collins Cobuild English Language Dictionary, 1987.
Collins Dictionary of the English Language, 2nd ed., 1986.
Compact Dictionary of Canadian English, 1970.
Concise Oxford Dictionary of Current English, 7th ed., 1982.

Dictionary of American English, 1938.
Dictionary of Americanisms, 1951.
Funk & Wagnalls New Standard Dictionary, 1949.
International English Usage, 1986.
Longman Dictionary of Contemporary English, 1978.
Longman Dictionary of the English Language, 1984.
Macquarie Dictionary, rev. ed., 1985.
Oxford Advanced Learner's Dictionary, 3rd ed., 1974.
Oxford English Dictionary, 12 vols., 1933.
Oxford English Dictionary Supplement, 4 vols., 1972–86.
Oxford Reference Dictionary, 1986.
Reader's Digest Great Illustrated Dictionary, 2 vols., 1984.
Webster's Ninth New Collegiate Dictionary, 1984.
Webster's Third New International Dictionary, 1961.

Seven key terms appear in many of those dictionaries: *Americanism, Australianism, Briticism, Canadianism, Hibernicism, Irishism*, and *Scotticism*. An additional nine terms were investigated in one dictionary each, for the sake of comparison: *Anglicism, Atticism, Celticism, Gallicism, Grecism, Hebraism, Hellenism, Latinism*, and *Yankeeism*.

A typical definition is something like the following concocted example for *Americanism*, with bracketed numbers added for later reference:

a [1] usage of language [2] characteristic of [3] the United States, [4] esp. as contrasted with that of England.

The definitions have four varying parts. The first is [1] the referential focus, or genus—in the example definition, "a usage of language." It is followed by a threefold distinguishing factor, or differentia, beginning with [2] the type of distinction—in the example, "characteristic of"—followed by [3] the geographical area—"United States." And last, [4] the standard of contrast—in the example, "as contrasted with that of England."

All four parts of the definition vary, not only from one dictionary to another, which might be expected, but also from one term to another within the same dictionary. For example, the *Oxford Reference Dictionary* defines *Americanism* as "a word, sense, or phrase peculiar to or originating in the USA" and *Briticism* as "an idiom used in Britain but not in the USA etc." The words chosen for those two definitions are interesting for both their denotations and their connotations. There seem to be more Americanisms of more kinds ("a word, sense, or phrase") than Briticisms ("an idiom"). Americanisms are "peculiar" and are innovations ("originating in"); Briticisms are simply "used in Britain," with the implication that they have always been there.

The Reader's Digest Great Illustrated Dictionary neatly reverses the prejudicial implications of the *Oxford Reference* by defining *Americanism* as "a usage of language characteristic of American English" and *Briticism* as "a word, phrase, or idiom characteristic of or peculiar to English as it is spoken in Great Britain." It is perhaps not wholly irrelevant that the *Great Illustrated* is based on the lexicographical data base of the Houghton Mifflin company of America.

It is clear that some dictionaries have made little effort to define nationalisms consistently as members of a semantic field. In such dictionaries, the terms seem rather to have been defined independently of each other in an ad hoc way. That fact is significant in suggesting that careful thought has not been given to the question of what constitutes a nationalism. Both in how they differ from one another and in the actual features chosen, the seventy definitions serve to highlight certain problems in our concept of a nationalism.

A caution about numbers, however: a given entry may express one part of the definition in several ways. For example, the referential focus may be "a word or phrase" or "an expression, phrase, construction, or idiom." Or the type of distinction may be "characteristic of or originating in." Because of such multiple expressions within a single part of the definition, the numbers reported hereafter for the variants in the referential focus and the type of distinction sometimes add up to more than seventy each.

The referential focus / The 70 entries include 120 specifications of referential focus. At its most general, the focus is expressed by terms like these (with the number of occurrences of each term in parentheses):

language (1)
usage (9)
feature (11)
expression (16)
mode of expression (3)
form of expression (1)

More specifically, many entries focus on the lexical aspects of national variation:

word (22)
phrase (17)
idiom (30)

The term *idiom* is, to be sure, ambiguous and might be interpreted either in a specifically lexical way, as 'an expression whose meaning cannot be predicted from the meanings of its parts,' or in a general sense, as 'a way of using language that is natural to a given group.' Because the term is thus ambiguous, it is unsuited for use in a definition, despite its popularity for that purpose.

Only a few entries specify particular levels of linguistic structure, such as phonological or orthographic variations:

pronunciation (1)
speech sound (1)
orthographical feature (1)

Equally few specify semantic variation:

sense (3)

Grammatical variation is also poorly represented, even supposing that the ambiguous term *construction* is to be understood in a grammatical, rather than a lexical, sense:

grammatical feature (1)
construction (2)

Finally, pragmatic matters of language are specified in only a single entry:

style (1)

National standards may differ from each other in any linguistic way. Between British and American there are differences in lexical items (*a wodge/mass of clouds*), phonology (*the SubSTANtive/ SUBstantive issue*), orthography (*jelly mould/jello mold*), grammar (*Wales were/was labeled an underdog, but they've made a nonsense of that/they've made nonsense of that*), semantics (*table a proposal* 'bring up for discussion'/'remove from discussion'), or pragmatics (—*What are you doing here? —I came to finish those letters, didn't I?* an aggressive putdown/a request for confirmation).

Because of the range of differences, general statements of referential focus are clearly more accurate than specific but incomplete ones. A Briticism or Americanism may be an expression, including its pronunciation, spelling, grammatical features, meaning, or applied use.

The type of distinction / The 70 entries include 85 specifications of the type of distinction. At their most general, the entries simply state that the focused features occur in the relevant geographical area. Such general expressions are the following:

used in/by (3)
as spoken in (1)
belonging to (2)
use of a national adjective without specification of the type of
    distinction, for example, *an American expression* (11)

Without further specification, such general terms provide no useful information. A linguistic feature "used in" one country, such as America, might also be used in all other English-speaking countries. Expressions of this sort imply something distinctive about the use, but do not specify what the distinction is. They are not definitions, but dodges.

A large number of definitions refer to a type of distinction that implies the feature is diagnostic of the area in question, by assisting an observer to identify the national variety:

characteristic of (33)
typical of (1)

Although a stronger statement than the preceding one, this is also vague in that it does not specify the way in which the feature is diagnostic. The unanswered question is: "Characteristic or typical in what way?"

One definition implies a statistical test, by which any feature that is more frequent in one national variety than another is a nationalism:

predominantly used by (1)

Another definition requires only that an association be made by observers between the linguistic feature and the national variety. On the basis of this definition, actual usage is less important than subjective judgment:

currently attributed to (1)

A considerably stronger relationship is implied by those several definitions that use the word *peculiar*. That word suggests 'possessed only by a particular group, unique':

peculiar to (21)
peculiarity (3)

A few definitions specify that the nationalism must have originated in the country in question. Others imply more specifically that it should have been a loan made in that country or have extended from there to other parts of the English-speaking world:

originating in (5)
originating from (1)
extending from (1)
borrowed into (1)

Historical records like the *Dictionary of Americanisms* may for their own purposes reasonably restrict the definition of a nationalism such as *Americanism* to items that originated in the country (the *DA*'s definition of that term being "a word or expression originating in the U.S."), but that is not the only way such terms are used.

Moreover, a considerable amount of confusion results from not clearly distinguishing the diachronic and the synchronic definitions of nationalisms. The *DA* itself is guilty of such confusion. It defines *Americanism* in accordance with its own stipulated use of the term as "a word or expression originating in the U.S." However, its first illustrative quotation is the 1781 use by Witherspoon cited above, which makes no mention of place of origin, but rather defines the term as denoting an expression with a use in America different from that in Great Britain. Thus the *DA* confuses its stipulated definition with one supported by its evidence.

All of the definitions of nationalisms fail to draw an important linguistic distinction between a word and its referent, either or both of which may be nationally limited. For example, Americans are generally unfamiliar with the British term *airing cupboard*; they are also unfamiliar with the thing it names, a heated closet in which garments or linens can be kept dry. Both word and thing are British.

On the other hand, Britons and Americans both have roads with dividing strips of land between the lanes of traffic going in opposite directions; Britons call them *dual carriageways* and Americans *divided highways*. The thing is international, but the words are nationalisms.

A third alternative is illustrated by the word *rook* for a type of crow. Many, perhaps most, Americans are familiar with the word from literary sources and know that it denotes a kind of large black bird; but the particular species denoted by the term, *Corvus frugilegus*, is not found in America naturally and so will be generally unfamiliar. The term is Common English, but the thing is un-American.

Airing cupboard and *dual carriageway* are clearly Briticisms. But what about *rook*? There is at least an argument that words, although widely known, are nationalisms if their referents are nationally restricted. In fact, nationalism terms are often used in just that way, *Briticism* being applied, for example, to *backbencher*, a word widely known in America, both through news reports and literature, but denoting a feature peculiar to parliamentary systems like that of England.

All the specific types of distinction mentioned above are reasonable grounds for identifying a nationalism. Thus a nationalism might be defined as an expression (pronunciation, spelling, grammatical feature, meaning, or use) that is peculiar to, used with greater frequency in, or associated for whatever reason with a particular nation, or that originated in or denotes a referent limited to that nation.

The geographical area / The area of use should be a trivial matter, being implicit in the term being defined. Thus *Canadianisms* are from Canada, *Australianisms* from Australia, and so forth. However, with the two most widely used national terms for English, *Americanism* and *Briticism*, the area creates a problem.

The problem is more acute with *Briticism*. In 13 definitions of that term, the statement of geographical area is variously expressed as follows:

Britain (3)
British (English) (3)
British Isles (1)
Great Britain (5)
Great Britain or the British (1)

Clearly these expressions were chosen to reflect the *Brit* morpheme in *Briticism*. The problem arises, however, in the definitions of those expressions. *Great Britain* and its short form *Britain* refer properly to England, Scotland, and Wales—and are so defined in most of the dictionaries that enter geographical terms.

However, *Collins* (1986) defines *Britain* as either 'Great Britain' or 'the United Kingdom', and the latter includes Northern Ireland in addition to the three historical nations of the main island.

The term *British Isles* includes all of Ireland and the Isle of Man, along with England, Scotland, and Wales.

Longman (1984) defines *British English* even more broadly: "English as spoken and written in Britain and in areas influenced by British culture—often taken to include that of parts of the Commonwealth." A literal interpretation of the *Longman* definition would make American English a part of British, since certainly British culture influenced that of the United States, being its origin. However, even when interpreted as its writers surely intended it, that definition extends *British English* to unspecified parts of the Commonwealth.

On the other hand, the two Merriam-Webster dictionaries define *British English* as "the native language of most inhabitants of England," a narrower interpretation than any of the others. Thus, according to the definitions of several dictionaries, *Briticism* can be understood as denoting expressions used in—

England
England, Scotland, and Wales
England, Scotland, Wales, and Northern Ireland
England, Scotland, Wales, Ireland, and the Isle of Man
England, Scotland, Wales, and parts of the Commonwealth

To some extent, these variants may be the accidental result of lexicographical imprecision, but they also reflect the fuzzy semantic boundaries of the term and the linguistic sensitivity of those who speak the variety it is used to denote.

Leaving aside the perennial Irish problem, many Scots and Welsh are keenly sensitive to their own cultural identity and resist, vigorously if not virulently, being subsumed under the terms *English* or *England*. On the other hand, some of the English resent the use of the word *British* in place of *English*. I was once severely taken to task by an English gentlewoman and scholar who informed me that she was English, not British, except on her passport, and that my use of the term *British* immediately marked me as one who was not himself English. The latter remark was apparently intended as the ultimate put-down.

British English and *Briticism* in their larger senses are sometimes objected to on the grounds that they denote a fiction— Scottish English, Welsh English, Irish English, and "English English" all differing from one another in significant ways. That objection is worthless, however, for it can be made to the name of any language variety. American English consists of New England English, Southern-Coastal English, Southern-Mountain English, Inland-Northern English, and so on. "English English" consists of Kentish English, Yorkshire English, Cockney English, and so on. And even RP, unless we are willing to identify it simply with

Daniel Jones's own usage, is an abstraction from the speechways of a great many individuals, differing from one another in many respects.

All varieties are fictions, in the sense that they are abstractions from the only linguistic reality, which is a set of utterances made under particular circumstances. On the whole, *British English* and *Briticism* denote a useful fiction. Objections to them, like objections to the term *standard*, usually have political, rather than scholarly, motivations.

A few unsuccessful efforts have been made to concoct other terms for the English of the home island, such as Anthony Burgess's proposed *Britglish* (*American Speech* 57 [1982]: 197). The stuttering *English English* for the language of England proper, has not won wide favor.

The political sensitivities of Scottish and Welsh nationalists, of Ulster Unionists, and of Eire patriots are inextricably entangled with linguistic variables. Since, however, the notion of a standard language is closely linked with that of political independence and solidarity, *British English* and *Briticism* can be usefully understood, at the present time at least, as applying to the language of the United Kingdom: England, Scotland, Wales, and Northern Ireland.

The problem with *American* is somewhat different. In 17 dictionary definitions of *Americanism*, the statements of geographical area fall into two groups:

United States (of America) or US(A) (10)
America, American (English), or Americans (7)

Those dictionaries that define *America* or *American* generally make it clear that those terms refer to the United States. Thus there is no lexicographical disagreement about the meaning of the term.

The problem with the terms *American English* (or, à la Burgess, *Amerglish?*) and *Americanism* is in part related to the larger difficulty that we have no simple name for the country and hence no satisfactory adjective. The proper name, *The United States of America*, is awkward and long and has the internal grammar of a common noun phrase. It does not lend itself to the easy formation of an adjective to denote the people and language. Instead we make do with the ambiguous *American*.

America and *American* have multiple disadvantages. First, they are used also to denote the entire hemisphere of the Americas. Second, they are used by Hispanic Americans to denote the non-Anglo parts of the two continents. And third, there is uncertainty about whether or not they apply also to Canada, which has its own independent national standard, although on the whole Canadian English is closer to that of the United States than to that of Britain. Nevertheless, the terms have been generally adopted for reference to the United States and its variety of English. And the various alternatives for the country suggested over the years, such as *Columbia, Freedonia, Alleghania, Appalachia,* and *Usona* have not been taken seriously.

In addition, words acquire associations. Allen Walker Read (*American Speech* 25 [1950]: 280–89) has documented what he calls the "pragmatic dimension" of the term *American* as it has been used in England through the years. Its connotative value has fluctuated with the level of political and cultural relations between the two countries, but even during relatively cordial times it has been "a synonym for barbarism . . . something to be disliked, to be avoided, and oftentimes to be hated" (as an American journalist put it in 1877). In 1891 a Canadian visitor to London described her conversation with an upper-class Englishwoman:

> "It is very American!" she said; and I felt that Mrs. Portheris could rise to no more forcible a climax of disapproval. . . . So I only smiled as sweetly as I could, and said, "So am I." (cited by Read 280)

Nearly a hundred years later similar remarks are still to be encountered. In a Cranks restaurant in London recently, one English woman remarked to her luncheon companion, "It's *very* American, and it's creeping in all over the place!" What is creeping in is unimportant; the point is that it was from America and the speaker did not like it.

In addition to its negative emotional value, however, *American* is also voguish, being applied to a variety of products—American pancakes, ice cream, or doughnuts—that seem even more exotic to Americans than they may to the British. An American traveler in 1911 observed:

> In our honor they have christened something that they wanted to dispose of "American Ice Cream." It is a sort of custard, savoring neither of America, ice nor cream. (cited by Read 284)

This latter phenomenon—the inappropriate application of national names to items unknown in the namesake nation—is a linguistic universal. In America, french fries are a form of potato without connection to France, German chocolate cake (a mildly cocoa-flavored pastry) maligns one of the few nations of the world to put a proper value on the use of pure chocolate, and English muffins are neither muffins nor anything else an English person would recognize.

Whatever their emotional value, however, *American English* and *Americanism* are relatively unambiguous terms, applying to the language of the United States. Although Canadian English is, from a linguistic standpoint, less different from the English of Michigan than the latter is from that of Alabama, the separate political status of the northern dominion gives it a distinct national standard.

A similar problem exists in antipodean English. Australia and New Zealand share many linguistic features, and a common term for them, *Austral English*, has been recorded by *Webster's Third* (although not *Australism*). However, their separate political status makes different national standards of their varieties of English. The lexicographical lack of a term, such as *New-Zealandism*, for talking about the features of that standard presumably reflects a gap in use and perceived need.

A term for the English shared by countries where it is spoken natively has also been hard to come by. The ambiguity of unmodified *English* has already been noted. The early volumes of *American Speech* (e.g., 5 [1929–30]: 175, 297–300, 414–16) had a large number of observations on various uses of the expression *Anglo-Saxon*. Among those uses is to denote 'English, British or American, of the present-day.' In addition, *Saxon* alone has been, and *Anglo* alone still often is, used in the same sense. *Mid-Atlantic English* has been used for what is in common to British and American, and terms like *World English* and *International English* have been used to include farther-flung varieties. *Core English* and *Common English* are relatively clear and self-explanatory terms.

The existence of such terminological problems exacerbates the difficulty of defining some terms for nationalisms.

The standard of contrast / This last part of the definition is lexicographically optional, being present in only 17 of the 70 entries. Though the statement of a standard of contrast is optional in lexicographical practice, the concept is an essential part of the meaning of terms for nationalisms.

For terms like *Gallicism, Grecism, Hellenism,* and *Latinism,* which denote the influence of one language on another, the standard of contrast is cross-linguistic and is something like the following:

esp. as used by a speaker or writer in another language (5)

Such terms and comparisons are parallel to, but quite distinct from, those that apply to nationalisms.

The comparison between terms for national standards may be a historical one:

now obsolescent or obsolete in (1)

Or it may be a synchronic, but categorical one, expressed in some way like the following:

but not used in (4)

Or it may be synchronic and imprecise (unless the precision is given elsewhere in the definition):

as contrasted with (7)

A given national variety may be contrasted with all other forms of English, as an overall pattern or a common core, or with another single national variety from which it most needs to be differentiated (as American and British from each other). For example, British English may be contrasted with the English used everywhere else in the world, so that Briticisms are either uses not found anywhere outside Britain (and thus peculiar to Britain) or uses not found everywhere outside Britain (and thus lacking from the common core of English though perhaps found in British and a number of other national varieties). Alternatively British English may be defined by comparing it with only one other national variety—American.

That British and American should be defined in relation to each other, without regard to the various other national varieties (Australian, Canadian, etc.), can be defended on a number of grounds. British and American were the first two national varieties to come into existence; as suggested above, they both originated at the same time, when parent English divided as a result of the American settlement and revolution. Historically, all other varieties are developments of one of these two and can consequently be conveniently related to them. They have the largest number of speakers of all native varieties. They are the widest spread of all varieties and the most influential in world use. Also as a practical matter, it is easier to compare one variety with another single variety rather than with all other varieties.

Drawing on the conclusions in the various parts of the preceding discussion, the definition of a nationalism might be something like this:

a linguistic feature (of pronunciation, spelling, grammar, meaning, or pragmatic use) that is unique to, occurs with greater frequency in, or is associated for whatever reason with a particular nation, in contrast to the usage of the same language in another nation, or that originated in the particular nation or denotes a referent limited to that nation.

Somewhat simplifying that schema and applying it to a specific national variety, British English, produces a definition like this:

Briticism: any linguistic feature of English that is unique to, occurs more often in, or is associated with the United Kingdom, in contrast to American English, or that originated in the United

Kingdom after the settlement of America, or that denotes a referent limited to the United Kingdom.

Such a definition is overexplicit for most lexicographical purposes. Dictionaries, after all, are written for the people who use them and who want their information to be handy and brief, even at the expense of completeness and exactness.

However, most dictionaries need a more consistent definition schema for nationalism terms than they now have. The lexicographer also needs a clearer concept of what constitutes a nationalism, even if the statement of that concept is fudged in writing practical definitions. For particular purposes, the lexicographer may well decide that parts of the schema are inappropriate. But such decisions need to be made with an awareness of how the term has been used and defined by others.

To a remarkable extent, standard English is one the world over. Yet variations there are, and national varieties. We cannot decide what is to count as a variation belonging to a national variety until we have defined the metalanguage we use to talk about them. These pages are a small essay in that direction, written in honor of a scholar who has molded our concept of what it means to talk about a standard.

Sociolinguistic Constraints
on Language Change
and the Evolution of *Are*
in Early Modern English

Guy Bailey

Long before the term "sociohistorical linguistics" gained currency, John Fisher had been laying the foundation for just such a discipline. His work on the evolution of Chancery English not only establishes the "social motivation" for standardization, but it also suggests a number of general constraints on language change.[1] In locating the emergence of the standard in the development of English as a written administrative language within Chancery, Fisher shows that language change is motivated as much by broad social, cultural, and political developments as by language contact and cleavages within social classes. In identifying the emerging written standard specifically with administrative English, he demonstrates how the uses of a language can affect language change. Thus the need for clarity and directness in administrative prose is an impetus for the development of hypotactic as opposed to paratactic structure. Further, in locating the evolving standard within Chancery, Fisher illustrates the importance of social networks in the diffusion of language change.[2] The relatively closed society formed by the twelve clerks and the specialized system of education within their households for minor clerks provided the kind of dense social network which reinforces and solidifies linguistic norms, while the ties between Chancery and Oxford and between Chancery and other civil servants such as Chaucer and Gower provided the kinds of weak links between networks that lead to the spread of language changes. Finally, in identifying the standard as a written language not based on any one spoken dialect, Fisher shows that written language is not simply the graphic representation of speech but is a separate code that changes and evolves independent of developments in the spoken language.

Each of these constraints on language change still operates. In fact, three of them have been crucial in the evolution of the Black English Vernacular (BEV) in the United States over the last seventy-five years. For example, work by Bailey and Maynor has shown how large-scale cultural and demographic developments, rather than language contact or class cleavages, have provided a social context for dramatic changes in the BEV, including the emergence of invariant *be* (as in *they be doing the breaking in PE and during class*) as a marker of durative/habitual aspect.[3] These developments stem largely from the Great Migration, a movement of blacks from the rural South into the urban North triggered by labor shortages in northern factories, the result of the military draft during World War I. Because it paralleled the movement of whites to the suburbs, the Great Migration eventually created cities within cities, islands where blacks often had little contact with whites and where spatial segration was much greater than in the rural South. The linguistic consequence of these social developments was the formation of distinct black speech communities (much as the Chancery formed a distinct language community) in which the language evolved without the influence of white speech. Further, in the cities blacks, like the Chancery, formed dense social networks where linguistic norms were strongly reinforced; the use of BEV in distinctive speech events and speech acts such as "the dozens" provided even more reinforcement. Finally, as some blacks moved back and forth between cities or between cities and smaller towns, they became the weak links between networks responsible for the diffusion of linguistic innovations.

The situation of BEV, of course, differs from that of Chancery English in several ways. For one thing, BEV is solely oral, Chancery English solely written. For another, the evolution of BEV represents the development of a nonstandard language, the evolution of Chancery English the development of a standard one.

Table *1*. *Plural Forms of the Present Tense of* BE *Used by the Younger Celys*

	be	ben	beth	is	are	Totals
Richard	26 (49%)	0	0	7 (13%)	20 (38%)	53
George	6 (21%)	6 (21%)	7 (25%)	8 (29%)	1 (4%)	28
William	76 (58%)	4 (3%)	9 (7%)	28 (21%)	15 (11%)	132

Source: Hanham

Nevertheless, the similarities indicate that the principles which emerge from John Fisher's work are in fact general constraints on language change and that standarization is simply a special instance of such change.[4] While these constraints provide a clear picture of some of the social mechanisms involved in language change, the linguistic mechanisms involved in change, and especially in grammatical change, are less clear. The unresolved question is this: when two grammatical forms are of equal social prestige, why (or, perhaps, how) is it that one displaces or comes to be preferred over another? In other words, what linguistic or cognitive factors lead speakers (or writers) to use one form instead of another?

The evolution of *are*, originally just a northern dialect form, as the present tense plural of *to be* in standard English is a good example of a grammatical change which, at least initially, seems not to have been motivated primarily by social factors. As Fisher, Richardson, and Fisher note, *be*, *ben* and *been* were the dominant plural forms in Chancery English: in fact, *are* occurs in only eight of the manuscripts in *An Anthology of Chancery English* and never more than once in any one manuscript.[5] As late as the end of the fifteenth century *be* was still the dominant plural form in the south of England. Thus in Hanham's edition of Cely letters written between 1472 and 1488, *be* accounts for 58 percent of the plural tokens in the present tense of *be*, with *are* accounting for only 13 percent (*ben*, *beth*, and *is* make up the remainder).[6] However, while *be* predominates throughout the letters, the encroachment of *are* is already apparent. Hanham points out that

*Table 2. Plural Forms Used by William Cely during Three Different
Time Periods*

	be	*are*	*others*	*Totals*
1479–82	42 (74%)	1 (2%)	14 (25%)	57
1483–84	27 (54%)	5 (10%)	18 (36%)	50
1487–88	7 (28%)	9 (36%)	9 (36%)	25

Source: Hanham

although the oldest generation of Celys consistently uses *be* as a
plural, the younger generation is quite varied in its usage except
for Robert, who has only *ben*. As Table 1 indicates, others of
the younger generation use five different plural forms. While *be*
accounts for about half of the tokens, the variety of forms clearly
shows the disintegration of the earlier consistent pattern and the
gradual encroachment of *are*. This encroachment is shown even
more clearly in Table 2, which provides a breakdown of plural
forms used by William Cely during three different time periods.
These data suggest that by the end of the fifteenth century, the
replacement of *be* by *are* was well under way.

Even as early grammars of English confirm that *be* was a common plural form and clearly regarded as standard, they also document the steady encroachment of *are*.[7] For example, the early
grammars of Du Wes (1532) and Thomas (1550) give only *be* as
the plural form of *to be*, while later sixteenth-century grammarians list *be* and *are* as alternative forms. It is not until Le Mayre's
The Dutch School-Master, published in 1606, that any grammar
gives *are* as the only plural, but after 1550 no grammarian gives
only *be*, although in the seventeenth century most grammars still
list *are* and *be* as alternative forms. While some grammarians,
including Bishop Lowth, continued to list *are* and *be* as alternative forms as late as the middle of the eighteenth century, the
use of *be* was becoming archaic by that time, as Lowth himself
indicates.[8] By the end of the eighteenth century it had become
solely a regional dialect form, restricted to the folk speech of the
West Country. In fact, James Buchanan, in *The British Gram-*

mar (1762), provides evidence that as early as the middle of the eighteenth century *be* as a plural indicative was already becoming stigmatized: he warns explicitly against its use. In a period of 250 years, then, a standard English form, predominant in the Chancery documents and clearly sanctioned in the grammars and usage guides of the day, became restricted to regional dialects, replaced by a form which itself had originally been restricted in much the same way. Although it seems clear that immigrants from the North brought *are* with them, that does not explain why native southerners gradually abandoned *be* in favor of the northern dialect form. Rather, the change from *be* to *are* seems to have little social motivation; as a result, it may offer some insight into the linguistic mechanisms of grammatical change.

While the Chancery records, the Cely letters, early grammars, and other sources clearly document the change from *be* to *are*, they do not in themselves provide evidence on the mechanism of change, information as to how and why the change took place. In fact, the only way of approaching this problem is by examining it in light of on-going grammatical changes in current varieties of English. A particularly useful variety for making such a comparison is BEV. Just as many of the same social constraints that affected Chancery English have affected it, BEV has also undergone (and is still undergoing) remarkable developments in the plural of the present tense of *be*.

THE DEVELOPMENT OF THE PRESENT TENSE OF *Be* IN *BEV*

The data for this discussion of the present tense of *be* in BEV come from mechanical recordings with three groups of lower-class black informants.[9] The first group includes twenty children, born between 1972 and 1975, who live in Bryan, Texas, the major urban area in the Brazos Valley region of East-Central Texas. Twenty-three adults born between 1890 and 1930, most of them tenant farmers or the wives of tenants in the Brazos Valley, make up the second group. The third group of informants pro-

Table 3. Plural Forms of the Present Tense of Be *Used in Three Varieties of BEV*

	be	is	are	Ø	Totals
Children	73 (28%)	24 (9%)	36 (14%)	130 (49%)	263
Adults	44 (6%)	139 (19%)	137 (19%)	407 (56%)	727
Ex-Slaves	4 (6%)	18 (19%)	17 (18%)	55 (58%)	94

Source: Bailey

vide our most important evidence on the structure of early BEV. In researching the early history of BEV, Bailey and Maynor discovered that the Library of Congress had a set of recordings made primarily during the 1930s and 1940s with former slaves born between 1844 and 1864 and was willing to make those recordings available. Further, about half of the evidence on the recordings came from Texas informants, and the two informants for whom the most data exists were from the Brazos Valley. When taken in conjunction with the other data from the Brazos Valley, these recordings provide evidence on the speech of informants who span 130 years in one place and provide unique insights into the early history of BEV.

The data from the elderly adults and former slaves are remarkably similar. As Table 3 shows, these informants use a variety of forms for the plural of the present tense of *be*, but the same forms occur with almost equal frequencies in both groups. In each the most common plural is the zero copula, as in

(1)   they bringing them in everyday;
(2)   and you think sometimes you pitiful. . . .

Are and *is* each account for about a fifth of the tokens, while *be* accounts for only 6 percent. Sentences such as the following, then, are relatively uncommon:

(3)   now children, they don't be happy lessen they walking the streets;
(4)   . . . they just be out to make money.

In addition to its low frequency of occurrence, *be* differs from the other plural forms in one more way. The occurrences of zero

Table 4. Syntactic Constraints on Present-Tense Forms in the Plural and Second- and Third-Person Singular in BEV (each form as a percentage of the total number of tokens in a given environment)

	v + ing	gonna	adj.	loc.	NP
Black Children					
is/are	14	11	73	67	86
be	44	0	2	13	2
Ø	41	89	25	19	12
Black Adults					
is/are	34	27	82	73	91
be	1	0	3	8	1
Ø	65	73	15	20	8
Ex-Slaves					
is/are	29	0	69	77	87
be	0	0	2	8	1
Ø	71	100	29	15	12

Source: Bailey

copula and the conjugated forms *are* and *is* seem to be influenced by what follows, as Table 4 indicates.[10] When a present participle or *gonna* follows, Ø generally occurs (more than two-thirds of the time). When a predicate adjective, locative, or noun phrase follows, however, the conjugated forms are more likely to be used (more than 70 percent of the time). Thus zero copula tends to occur as the auxiliary, the conjugated forms as the copula. As Table 4 again suggests, no such patterning affects *be*: it is simply an occasional variant of both the auxiliary and copula, a kind of "spare form."

In the speech of the children, on the other hand, the situation is remarkably different. Table 3 indicates that the same forms used in the earlier varieties also occur in the speech of the children, but it also shows a dramatic increase in the use of *be*, which occurs more than four times as often as it does in the speech of the adults and former slaves. However, the frequency of *be* does not increase in all environments. As Table 4 shows, the greater use of *be* takes place almost entirely before present participles: elsewhere the distribution of *be* remains virtually unchanged. Further, in the speech of the children *be* is actually the most common plural before present participles.

At first glance, the sudden increase in the use of *be* as the form before present participles seems odd. Why should there be a dramatic increase in the use of *be* in only one environment? If the increase occurred in all or even most of the environments, age-grading (the greater use of nonstandard forms by children) would seem a likely explanation. However, except before present participles, the frequency of *be* is quite similar in all three varieties. Other social factors are also of little use in explaining the high frequency of *be*: all of the informants come from the same social class, and most are from the same part of Texas. As with the shift from *are* to *be* in Early Modern English, then, this development in BEV seems to be a grammatical change which has little social motivation.[11] In fact, a closer examination of the grammatical and semantic constraints on the use of *be* suggests that its increased use was motivated largely by internal linguistic factors.

A clue to the greater use of *be* before present participles lies in the semantics of the English progressive, the structure created by some form of *to be* followed by a present participle. As a number of linguists have pointed out, the English progressive actually signals much more than progressive aspect: it can in fact signal a number of meanings that are not "progressive" at all.[12] In addition to actions in progress, the English progressive can also be used to refer to future, habitual, and continuous activities, as in

(5)   I'm leaving Wednesday;
(6)   I'm lifting weights twice a week;
(7)   I'm growing older.

An analysis of all of the progressives in our data suggests that the more frequent use of *be* before present participles by children is a response to these anomalies in the English progressive. As Table 5 indicates, the adults make no semantic distinctions among the forms used in the progressive: Ø dominates equally as a marker both of habitual and durative actions and of futures

Table 5. Meaning of Present-Tense Forms Before V + ing *in BEV*
(each form as a percentage of the total number of tokens in a given
environment)

	Limited Duration/Future	*Extended Duration/Habitual*
Children:		
is/are	29	3
be	5	77
Ø	65	20
Adults:		
is/are	21	20
be	0	6
Ø	79	73

Source: Bailey

and actions of limited duration (i.e., true progressives).[13] Among
children, the situation is quite different. Zero and the conjugated
forms are used to signal limited duration, the meaning typically
associated with the progressive, or to refer to future events. For
habitual and durative actions, on the other hand, *be* is clearly the
dominant form, accounting for over three quarters of the tokens
in these contexts. In the speech of the children, then, *be* seems
to have been reanalyzed as an auxiliary marking durative/habitual
aspect, contrasting systematically with Ø, which is used for true
progressives and for futures.

In an essay entitled "Syntactic Reanalysis," Robert Langacker
describes the linguistic process of reanalysis as a "change in the
structure of an expression or class of expressions that does not
involve any immediate or intrinsic modification of its surface
manifestation" (58). Although reanalysis itself is unobservable,
its effects can be observed as linguistic forms acquire new uses
and undergo significant changes in their distribution. This kind of
reanalysis has its motivation in tendencies toward what Langacker
calls "transparency . . . , the notion that the ideal or optimal
linguistic code, other things being equal, will be one in which
every surface unit . . . will have associated with it a clear, salient,

and reasonably consistent meaning or function, and every semantic element in a sentence will be associated with a distinct and recognizable surface form" (110). Further, reanalysis is generally a response to local structural pressure. One way that languages achieve such transparency is by eliminating meaningless forms or by assigning them new meanings.

Just such a process seems to have happened with *be* in recent BEV. The unusually wide semantic range of the English progressive provided the kind of local structural pressure that is the ideal grammatical context for reanalysis, while the occurrence of *be* as an unsystematic variant in both the auxiliary and the copula provided a grammatical form that had no unique meaning or function associated with it. The creation of distinct black speech communities as a result of the migration of blacks from the rural South to the urban areas, especially in the North, provided a social context in which these two factors could lead to reanalysis. The reanalysis of *be* as a marker of durative/habitual aspect represents a significant gain in transparency: it gives a unique, salient, and reasonably consistent function to *be*, and it makes the English progressive somewhat less messy as *be* is used with present participles to signal durative/habitual meanings while Ø and the conjugated forms are used to signal true progressives and future meanings. The movement toward transparency, then, seems to be the linguistic motivation for this grammatical change.

THE LINGUISTIC MOTIVATION
FOR THE RISE OF "ARE"

An examination of the various uses of *be* in Early Modern English suggests that the same principle of transparency may well have motivated the replacement of *be* by *are* as a plural. Although *be* was clearly the predominant form in the indicative plural at the beginning of the Early Modern English period, it had three additional functions as well. As in contemporary English, of course, it was the infinitive used after other verbs. However, it was also used as a subjunctive in conditional sentences, occurring especially after such subordinators as *if*, *although*, *though*, *unless*, and *except*, as the early grammarians indicate. Finally, Fisher, Richardson, and Fisher note in *An Anthology of Chancery English* that *be* was sometimes used where contemporary English required *been*, as in

(8)   it hath be used;

(9)   John Hull haath long tyme be.[14]

The situation with *be* in Early Modern English, then, was the exact opposite of that in early BEV. In BEV several forms, including *be*, served the same function; in Early Modern English a single form, *be*, served several functions. Both cases, however, represent a clear lack of transparency, with a mismatch between the number of forms and functions. BEV achieved greater transparency by reanalyzing *be*, thus constraining its function and distribution. Early Modern English, on the other hand, achieved greater transparency by borrowing the *are* which northern immigrants brought with them, using it for the indicative plural and restricting *be* to subjunctive and infinitival uses. As *are* gradually supplanted *be* in the indicative and *been* came to be the only perfect participial form, Early Modern English achieved significantly greater transparency by the middle of the eighteenth century. Thus the transparency principle provides the motivation for two different developments in the plural of the present tense of *be* in two widely separated varieties of English during two different periods of time. In one case a form was reanalyzed, in the other a form was borrowed, but the linguistic motivation underlying each was the same.

CONCLUSION

The comparison of the replacement of *be* by *are* in Early Modern English with the reanalysis of *be* in BEV demonstrates that the same processes that occur in nonstandard varieties also occur in standard ones and suggests that standardization is simply a special instance of language change. It also illustrates the linguistic motivation for the evolution of *are* in standard English. Although social developments provided the context for the change from *be* to *are*, those developments do not explain the change. Rather, the change reflects a movement toward transparency, toward a more optimal code wherein each surface unit has a distinct, recognizable form. While transparency is clearly not the only linguistic mechanism at work (if it were, there would be no messy linguistic systems in the first place), it does suggest the kinds of linguistic constraints we need to look for. An understanding of these constraints is crucial as we construct a theory of language change on the foundations laid by people such as John Fisher.

NOTES

1. The two most important works in providing this foundation for sociohistorical linguistics, of course, are *An Anthology of Chancery English*, edited with Malcolm Richardson and Jane Fisher, and "Chancery and the Emergence of Standard Written English in the Fifteenth Century." While both of these are crucial for work on the history of English, they are also of enormous value for more theoretical work on language variation and change and should prove a rich source of evidence for sociolinguists for years to come.

2. For a discussion of the importance of social networks in language change, see Lesley Milroy's *Language and Social Networks* and "Linguistic Change and the Ideal Speaker Hearer."

3. "Decreolization?" provides a more complete account of these developments and is the source for this discussion.

4. Cf. the similar conclusions reached by Peter Trudgill in *Dialects in Contact*.

5. The discussion here is based on the discussion of morphology in *An Anthology of Chancery English*.

6. These percentages are based on my tallies of occurrences of the various forms of *to be* in Hanham's *The Cely Letters, 1472–1488*. The data in Tables 1 and 2 are taken from her introduction.

7. This conclusion, as well as others about early grammars, is based on an examination of the more than three hundred works in the series *English Linguistics, 1500–1800*, edited by R.C. Alston.

8. In the first edition of *A Short Introduction to English Grammar*, Lowth lists *be* and *are* as alternative plurals without further comment. In the second edition he adds the note that *be* is antiquated in the plural and "wholly obsolete" in the singular.

9. A more complete discussion of methods and data and a more detailed analysis is provided in a series of articles by Bailey and Maynor, all of which are listed in the references.

10. Tables 4 and 5 also include data on the third singular. The reanalysis of *be* as an auxiliary of durative/habitual aspect makes *be* a systematic variant in that person/number as well.

11. That does not mean that social factors played no role at all. As we point out below, the Great Migration provided the social context within which grammatical change could take place. Likewise, immigration from the North to the South of England made *are* a possible variant in Early Modern English. In neither case, however, do social factors explain how or why the changes occurred.

12. See Comrie's *Aspect* both for a more complete discussion of the English progressive and for a comparison with more typical progressive aspects in other languages.

13. The data from the former slaves are not included in Table 5 since they do not use *be* before present participles.

14. Both examples are from *An Anthology of Chancery English*. Fisher, Richardson, and Fisher also provide a useful discussion of the various functions of *be* in Chancery English.

REFERENCES

Bailey, Guy. "Are Black and White Vernaculars Diverging?" *American Speech* 62 (1987), 32–40; 75–76.

Bailey, Guy and Natalie Maynor. "Decreolization?" *Language and Society* 16 (1987), 449–73.

———. "The Present Tense of *Be* in Southern Black Folk Speech." *American Speech* 60 (1985), 195–212.

———. "The Present Tense of *Be* in White Folk Speech of the Southern United States." *English World-Wide* 6 (1985), 199–216.

Buchanan, James. *The British Grammar*. Facsimile reprint of 1762 edition. Menston, England: The Scholar Press, 1968.

Comrie, Bernard. *Aspect*. Cambridge: Cambridge University Press, 1976.

Du Wes, Giles. *An Introduction For To Learn To Read, To Pronounce, and To Speak French*. Facsimile reprint of 1532 edition. Menston, England: The Scholar Press, 1972.

Fisher, John H. "Chancery and the Emergence of Standard Written English in the Fifteenth Century." *Speculum* 52 (1977), 870–99.

Fisher, John H., Malcolm Richardson, and Jane L. Fisher, eds. *An Anthology of Chancery English*. Knoxville: University of Tennessee Press, 1984.

Hanham, Alison, ed. *The Cely Letters, 1472–1488*. Early English Text Society No. 273. Oxford: Oxford University Press, 1975.

Le Mayre, Marten. *The Dutch School-Master*. Facsimile reprint of 1606 edition. Menston, England: The Scholar Press, 1977.

Lowth, Robert. *A Short Introduction to English Grammar*. Facsimile reprint of 1762 edition. Menston, England: The Scholar Press, 1967.

Milroy, Leslie. *Language and Social Networks*. Oxford: Basil Blackwell, 1980.

———. "Linguistic Change and the Ideal Speaker Hearer". Conference on The Social Context of Language Change. Paper read at Stanford University, 26 July 1987.

Thomas, William. *Principal Rules of the Italian Grammar*. Facsimile reprint of 1550 edition. Menston, England: The Scholar Press, 1968.

Trudgill, Peter. *Dialects in Contact*. Oxford: Basil Blackwell, 1986.

The Bibliography
of John Hurt Fisher
through 1987

Judith Law Fisher and Mark Allen

The bibliography of John Hurt Fisher is not complete without mention of his editorial work. As Executive Secretary of the Modern Language Association, he edited *PMLA* from 1963 through 1971, the *MLA Newsletter* from its inception in 1969 through 1971, and *MLA Abstracts* in 1971 and (with Walter Achtert) 1972. As President of the New Chaucer Society, he has also edited the *Chaucer Newsletter* since 1984.

BOOKS

The Tretyse of Loue. Early English Text Society, no. 223. London: Oxford University Press, 1951. Reprint. 1970.
This Man's Art. Edited with Edwin R. Hunter. Maryville, Tennessee: Maryville College, 1964.
John Gower: Moral Philosopher and Friend of Chaucer. New York: New York University Press, 1964.
The Medieval Literature of Western Europe, Mainly 1930–1960. General Editor. New York: New York University Press, 1966.
The MLA Style Sheet. 2d ed. Edited with others. New York: Modern Language Association, 1970.
In Forme of Speche is Chaunge: Readings in the History of the English Language. With Diane Bornstein. New York: Prentice-Hall, 1974. Reprint. Lanham, Maryland: University Press of America, 1984.
The Complete Poetry and Prose of Geoffrey Chaucer. New York: Holt, Rinehart and Winston, 1977. 7th printing with revised bibliography, 1981. This text of the *Canterbury Tales* appeared as the English text on facing pages of French translation, in *Les Contes de Cantorbéry,*

2ème partie, translated by Juliette de Caluwé-Dor (Louvain: Peeters, 1986).

An Anthology of Chancery English. With Malcolm Richardson and Jane L. Fisher. Knoxville: University of Tennessee Press, 1984.

The Essential Chaucer: An Annotated Bibliography of Major Modern Studies. With Mark Allen. Boston: G. K. Hall, 1987.

ARTICLES

"Primary and Secondary Education and the Presbyterian Church in the United States of America." *Journal of the Presbyterian Historical Society* 24 (1946):13–43.

"Continental Associations for the *Ancrene Riwle.*" *PMLA* 64 (1949): 180–89.

"On Attitudes Towards Language Study." *CEA Critic* 12 (1950):1, 5.

"Serial Bibliographies in the Modern Languages and Literatures." *PMLA* 66 (1951):138–56.

"Chaucer's Use of *Swete* and *Swote.*" *JEGP* 50 (1951):326–31.

"The Ancestry of the English Alphabet." *Archaeology* 4 (1951):232–42. Reprinted in *English Then and Now*, edited by Alan M. Markman and Erwin R. Steinberg, 77–88. New York: Random House, 1970.

"Seven Variants in the *Tretyse of Loue.*" *Publications of the Bibliographical Society of America* 46 (1952):393–96.

"We Look to the High Schools." *College English* 14 (1955):362–65.

"The Problems of Freshman Composition." *College Composition and Communication Conference Bulletin* 6 (1955):75–78.

"MLA Group Projects." *PMLA* 70 (1955):3–33.

"Tristan and Courtly Adultery." *Comparative Literature* 9 (1957):150–64.

"Certification of High School Teachers." *College English* 18 (1958): 344–48.

"The French Versions of the *Ancrene Riwle.*" In *Middle Ages—Reformation—"Volkskunde,"* 65–74. Festschrift for John G. Kunstmann. North Carolina University Studies in Germanic Languages and Literatures, no. 26. Chapel Hill: University of North Carolina Press, 1959.

"A Calendar of Documents Relating to the Life of John Gower." *JEGP* 58 (1959):1–23.

"Chaucer's Horses." *South Atlantic Quarterly* 60 (1961):71–80.

"Wyclif, Langland, Gower, and the *Pearl* poet on the Subject of Aristocracy." In *Studies in Medieval Literature: In Honor of Professor Albert Croll Baugh*, edited by MacEdward Leach, 139–57. Philadelphia: University of Pennsylvania Press, 1961.

"1960 Certification Requirements." *College English* 22 (1961):271–75.

"The New Interrelation Between First and Second Language Learning." *Reports of Surveys and Studies in the Teaching of Modern Foreign Languages*, 277–80. New York: Modern Language Association, 1961.

"New Perspectives on Teaching English." *Current Issues in Higher Education*, edited by G. Kerry Smith, 82–84. Washington, D.C.: NEA Association for Higher Education, 1962.

"Why a Conference of Chairmen?" *College English* 24 (1962):243–44.

"Embarrassment of Riches." *College Language Association Journal* 7 (1962):1–12.

Certification data in *The Education of Teachers of English*, edited by Alfred H. Grommon, 176–78, 213–17, 303. National Council of Teachers of English Curriculum Series, no. 5. New York: Appleton-Century-Crofts, 1963.

"The MLA in Wonderland." *South Atlantic Bulletin* 39 (March 1964): 1–4.

"Prospect." In *The College Teaching of English*, edited by John H. Fisher and Curt A. Zimansky, 1–11. National Council of Teachers of English Curriculum Series, no. 4. New York: Appleton-Century-Crofts, 1965.

Foreword to John S. Diekhoff. *The NDEA and Modern Foreign Languages*, ix–xii. New York: Modern Language Association, 1965.

"Editing *PMLA*." *College English* 27 (1965):147–49.

"MLA-NYU Spark Language Teaching Revolution." *The New York University Alumni Bulletin* 9 (April 1966):3, 8.

"English Education and College and University Departments of English." *CEE Newsletter* (National Council of Teachers of English) 4 (February 1966):4–8.

"Edwin Arlington Robinson and Arthurian Tradition." In *Studies in Language and Literature in Honour of Margaret Schlauch*, edited by Mieczysław Brahmer, Stanisław Helsztyński, and Julian Krzyżanowski, 117–31. Warsaw: Państwowe Wydawnictwo Naukowe, 1966.

"The Humanities in an Age of Science." *The Journal of General Education* 18 (1966):181–91.

Foreword to William G. Moulton. *Linguistics and Language Learning*, vii–viii. New York: Modern Language Association, 1966.

Foreword to William R. Parker. *The Language Curtain*, ix–xi. New York: Modern Language Association, 1966.

"The Progress of Research in Medieval English Literature in the United States of America." In *English Studies Today*, 4th series, edited by Ilva Cellini and Giorgio Melchiori, 33–45. Lectures and Papers Read at the Sixth Conference of the International Association of University Professors of English, Venice, 1965. Rome: Edizioni di Storia et Letteratura, 1966.

"The New English." *The Book of Knowledge Annual*, edited by Louise McDowell, 256–60. New York: Grolier, Inc., 1967.

"Language and the Expanding Humanities." *Journal of English as a Second Language* 2 (1967):17–25.

"Importance of the English Teacher Preparation Study." *English Journal* 54 (1968):477, 550.

"Progress of Scholarship in English in the United States." *Bulletin of the International Association of University Professors of English* (Spring 1968):20–22.

Foreword to Lawrence F. McNamee. In *Dissertations in English and American Literature*, vii. New York: R.R. Bowker, 1968.

"The Modern Language Association of America, 1883–1968." *American Council of Learned Societies Newsletter* 20 (March 1969):19–25.

"The MLA Editions of Major American Authors." In *Professional Standards and American Editions: A Response to Edmund Wilson*, 20–26. New York: Modern Language Association, 1969.

"Movement in English." *Association of Departments of English Bulletin*, no. 22 (September 1969):40–43.

"Why an ADFL?" *Association of Departments of Foreign Languages Bulletin* 1, no. 1 (September 1969):4.

"Language as Emblem." *School and Society* 97 (November 1969):446–49.

"The King's English in a Working Man's World." *Association of Departments of English Bulletin*, no. 26 (September 1970):17–20.

"Languages and Loyalty." *Association of Departments of Foreign Languages Bulletin* 2, no. 1 (September 1970):13–17.

"To Look Inward." *Association of Departments of Foreign Languages Bulletin* 3, no. 1 (September 1971):9–13.

"An Anthropological View of the Teaching of Literature." *Bulletin of the Rocky Mountain Modern Language Association* 25 (March 1971): 28–35.

"Chaucer's Last Revision of the *Canterbury Tales*." *Modern Language Review* 67 (1972):241–51.
"Facing Up to the Problems of Going Interdisciplinary." *Association of Departments of English Bulletin*, no. 32 (February 1972):5–9. Reprinted in *Prospects for the 70's*, 90–94. New York: Modern Language Association, 1973.
"Our Discovery of Diversity." *Association of Departments of English Bulletin*, no. 35 (December 1972):16–17.
"Jubilee Plus Three: The Founding of the MHRA and Its Early Relations With the MLA." *Annual Bulletin of the Modern Humanities Research Association* 44 (November 1972):18–28.
"Standard English From Printing Press to Magnetic Tape." In *Expression, Communication and Experience in Literature and Language*, edited by Ronald G. Popperwell, 212–15. Proceedings of the XII Congress of the International Federation of Modern Languages and Literatures, Cambridge University, August, 1972. [London]: Modern Humanities Research Association, [1972].
"Truth versus Beauty: An Inquiry Into the Function of Language and Literature in an Articulate Society." National Council of Teachers of English Distinguished Lecture, 1972. Audio Cassette. Champaign, Ill.: National Council of Teachers of English, 1972. Printed in *The Humanity of English*, 1–16. Champaign, Ill.: National Council of Teachers of English, 1972. Reprinted in *The English Journal* 62 (1973):205–14.
"Notes on the Place of English in American Culture." *The Pennsylvania Council of Teachers of English Bulletin* 27 (April 1973):3–7.
"The Three Styles of Fragment I of the *Canterbury Tales*." *Chaucer Review* 8 (1973):119–27.
"The Dancer and the Dance." Modern Language Association Presidential Address. *PMLA* 90 (1975):361–65.
"The Law and the English Language." In *Your Laws: Your Right to Know*, 27–36. Knoxville: University of Tennessee Press, 1975.
"The Intended Illustrations in Ms. Corpus Christi 61 of Chaucer's *Troylus and Criseyde*." In *Medieval Studies in Honor of Lillian Herlands Hornstein*, edited by Jess B. Bessinger, Jr., and Robert R. Raymo, 111–22. New York: New York University Press, 1976.
"Nationalism Versus Internationalism as a Rationale for the Study of Literature." In *Language and Literature in the Formation of National and Cultural Communities*, edited by Robert D. Eagleson, Robert

White, and Christopher Bentley, 186–88 (abstract). Proceedings of the XIII Congress of the Fédération Internationale des Langues et Littératures Modernes and the XVII Congress of the Australasian Universities Language and Literature Association. Sydney: AULLA, 1976.

"The Administration and the Curriculum." *South Atlantic Association of Departments of English Newsletter* 5, no. 1 (June 1977).

"The Myth of Petrarch." In *Jean Misrahi Memorial Volume: Studies in Medieval Literature*, edited by Hans R. Runte, Henri Niedzielski, and William L. Hendrickson, 359–73. Columbia, S.C.: French Literature Publications, 1977.

"Chancery and the Emergence of Standard Written English in the Fifteenth Century." *Speculum* 52 (1977):870–99.

"Standard English in Its Historical Context." *North Carolina English Teacher* 35 (1977):19–26.

"The Revision of the Prologue to the *Legend of Good Women*." *South Atlantic Bulletin* 43, no. 4 (1978):75–84.

"Defining the Humanities." *Cross Reference* (Tennessee Committee on the Humanities) 1 (Winter 1978):4.

"The *Legend of Good Women*." In *Companion to Chaucer Studies*, 2d ed., edited by Beryl Rowland, 464–76. New York: Oxford University Press, 1979.

"Chancery Standard and Modern Written English." *Journal of the Society of Archivists* 6 (1979):136–44.

"An Annotated Chaucer Bibliography, 1976–77." *Studies in the Age of Chaucer* 1 (1979):201–55.

"Nationalism and the Study of Literature." *American Scholar* 49 (Winter 1979–80):105–10.

"Scala Chauceriensis." In *Approaches to Teaching Chaucer's Canterbury Tales*, edited by Joseph Gibaldi, 39–45. New York: Modern Language Association, 1980.

"An Annotated Chaucer Bibliography, 1977–78." *Studies in the Age of Chaucer* 2 (1980):221–85.

"Business, Culture, and the History of Standard Language." In *No More Elegies: Essays in the Future of the Humanities*, edited by Clifford Earl Ramsey, 1–12. Federation Resources, no. 8. Minneapolis, Minn.: Federation of Public Programs in the Humanties, 1980.

"An Annotated Chaucer Bibliography, 1979." *Studies in the Age of Chaucer* 3 (1981):189–259.

"School English and Public Policy." *College English* 43 (1981):856–57.

"Language, Manners, Laws, and Customs." *SCETC Newsletter* 14 (Fall 1981):6–12.

"Chaucer and the French Influence." In *New Perspectives in Chaucer Criticism*, edited by Donald M. Rose, 177–92. Norman, Okla.: Pilgrim Books, 1981.

"English Literature." In *The Present State of Scholarship in Fourteenth-Century Literature*, edited by Thomas D. Cooke, 26–54. Columbia: University of Missouri Press, 1982.

"An Annotated Chaucer Bibliography, 1980." *Studies in the Age of Chaucer* 4 (1982):193–246.

"Chaucer's Prescience." New Chaucer Society Presidential Address. *Studies in the Age of Chaucer* 5 (1983):3–16.

"The Symbiosis of Speech and Writing." In *Adjoining Cultures as Reflected in Literature and Language*, edited by John X. Evans and Peter Horwath, 37–52. Proceedings of the XVth Congress of the Fédération Internationale des Langues et Littératures Modernes. Tempe: Arizona State University, 1983.

"Remembrance and Reflection." *PMLA* (Centennial Issue) 99 (1984): 398–407.

"Introductory Remarks, MLA Centennial Forum." *PMLA* 99 (1984): 996–1004, passim.

"Caxton and Chancery English." In *Fifteenth-Century Studies*, edited by Robert F. Yeager, 161–85. New Haven, Conn.: Archon Books, 1984.

"Chaucer and Written Language." In *The Popular Literature of Medieval England*, edited by Thomas J. Heffernan, 237–51. Tennessee Studies in Literature, no. 28. Knoxville: University of Tennessee Press, 1985.

"John Gower." With Wayne Hamm, Peter G. Beidler, and Robert F. Yeager. In *A Manual of Writings in Middle English, 1050–1500*, edited by A.E. Hartung, 7:2195–2234, 2399–2418. New Haven: Connecticut Academy of Arts and Sciences, 1986.

"European Chancelleries and the Rise of Standard Languages." *Proceedings of the Illinois Medieval Association* 3 (1986):1–33.

"Middle English Literature." In *Dictionary of the Middle Ages*, edited by Joseph R. Strayer, 8:313–26. New York: Charles Scribner's Sons, 1987.

REVIEWS

D. W. Lee, *Functional Change in Early English*, in *Word* 6 (1950): 190–92.

A. Rynell, *Rivalry in Scandinavian and English Synonyms*, in *Word* 6 (1950):247–48.

Morton Bloomfield, *The Seven Deadly Sins*, in *Speculum* 28 (1953): 863–65.

R. F. Jones, *The Triumph of the English Language*, in *17th Century News* 12 (1954):10–11.

Joseph T. Shipley, *Dictionary of Early English*, in *Renaissance News* 9 (1956):98–100.

F. M. Salter, *Medieval Drama in Chester*, in *Modern Language Notes* 72 (1957):50–52.

K. L. Wood Legh, *A Small Household of the Fifteenth Century*, in *Renaissance News* 10 (1957):98–100.

E. J. F. Arnould, *The Melos Amoris of Richard Rolle*, in *Speculum* 33 (1958):373–75.

M. B. Salu, *The Ancrene Riwle*, in *Modern Language Notes* 73 (1958): 639–40.

A. S. Diamond, *History and Origin of Language*, in *South Atlantic Quarterly* 59 (1960):584–86.

H. Sands, *Caxton's Reynard the Fox*, in *JEGP* 60 (1961):576.

Joseph A. Lauritis, Ralph A. Klinefelter, and Vernon F. Gallagher, *Lydgate's Life of Our Lady*, in *Yearbook of Comparative Literature* 10 (1961):91–92.

Eric Stockton, trans., *The Major Latin Poems of John Gower*, in *English Language Notes* 1 (September 1963):59–61.

William Matthews, *The Tragedy of Arthur: A Study of the Alliterative Morte Arthure*, in *The Historian* 23 (1963):491–92.

John Lawler, ed., *Patterns of Love and Courtesy: Essays in Honor of C.S. Lewis*, in *Modern Language Review* 63 (1968):162–63.

Charles Muscatine, *Poetry and Crisis in the Age of Chaucer*, in *South Atlantic Quarterly* 72 (1973):609–11.

Council of Graduate Schools Reports, *Alternative Approaches to Graduate Study*, in *Association of Departments of English Bulletin*, no. 41 (May 1974):19–21.

Robert W. Frank, *The Legend of Good Women*, in *Modern Philology* 72 (1975):292–94.

David L. Jeffrey, *The Early English Lyrics and Franciscan Spirituality*, in *JEGP* 75 (1976):588–89.

Marcelle Thiébaux, *The Stag of Love: The Chase in Medieval Literature*, in *Speculum* 52 (1977):437–39.

Dorothee Metlitzki, *The Matter of Araby in Medieval England*, in *JEGP* 76 (1977):539–41.

Charles Moorman, ed., *The Works of the Gawain Poet*, in *Speculum* 53 (1978):833–35.

Charles A. Owen, Jr., *Pilgrimage and Storytelling in the Canterbury Tales*, in *Speculum* 53 (1978):835–36.

Walter Kaufman, *The Future of the Humanities*, in *South Atlantic Quarterly* 77 (1978):524–25.

Peggy Ann Knapp, *The Style of John Wyclif's English Sermons*, in *Speculum* 54 (1979):161–62.

Anthony G. Petti, *English Literary Hands from Chaucer to Dryden*, in *Speculum* 54 (1979):183–84.

John M. Fyler, *Chaucer and Ovid*, in *Speculum* 55 (1980):866.

J. D. Burnley, *Chaucer's Language and the Philosopher's Tradition*, in *Speculum* 56 (1981):448–49.

Niel D. Smyser and Robin Content, *The Changing Academic Market Place*, in *College English* 43 (1981):838–40.

N. F. Blake, ed., *The Canterbury Tales*, in *Analytical and Enumerative Bibliography* 5 (1981):160–62.

René Cappon, *The Word: An Associated Press Guide to Good News Writing*, in *Associated Press Managing Editors Association News* (July 1983):6.

Dennis E. Baron, *Grammar and Good Taste: Reforming the American Language*, in *American Literature* 55 (1983):671–73.

V. A. Kolve, *Chaucer and the Imagery of Narrative*, in *JEGP* 84 (1985): 415–17.

A. J. Minnis, ed., *Gower's Confessio Amantis: Responses and Reassessments*, in *Studies in the Age of Chaucer* 7 (1985):221–24.

Paul G. Ruggiers, ed., *Editing Chaucer: The Great Tradition*, in *Studies in the Age of Chaucer* 8 (1986):239–41.

RECORDINGS

"Examples of Old English, Middle English, and Early Modern English." Macmillan Linguistics Laboratory, 1972.

Contributors

JOHN ALGEO is Professor of English at the University of Georgia, where he has served as department head and as director of the linguistic program. During the academic year 1986–87, he was a Guggenheim Fellow and Fulbright Research Scholar at the Survey of English Usage, University College London. Among his many books are *Origins and Development of the English Language* (with Thomas Pyles), *On Defining the Proper Name*, and *Exercises in Contemporary English*. He served as editor of *American Speech* for ten years, and he is currently editing "Among the New Words" for *American Speech* and preparing *A Dictionary of Briticisms*.

MARK ALLEN is Assistant Professor of English in the Division of English, Classics, and Philosophy at the University of Texas at San Antonio. He has published in the fields of Old and Middle English and fantasy literature, most recently in *Studies in the Age of Chaucer*, and, with John H. Fisher, *The Essential Chaucer: An Annotated Bibliography of Major Modern Studies*.

GUY BAILEY is Associate Professor of English at Texas A&M University. He is author of *A Social History of the Gulf States* and co-author of a number of monographs in the Linguistic Atlas of the Gulf States. He is co-editor with Michael Montgomery of *Language Variety in the South: Perspectives in Black and White*.

N. F. BLAKE is Professor of English Language and Head of the Department of English Language at the University of Sheffield and is currently serving as Pro-Vice-Chancellor of that University. He has written or edited eighteen books among the best known of which are his edition of the Hengwrt Manuscript of *The Canterbury Tales, Caxton and His World, The*

Textual Tradition of The Canterbury Tales, Non-Standard Language in English Literature, and *Shakespeare's Language: an Introduction.*

J. D. BURNLEY is Senior Lecturer in English Language at the University of Sheffield. He is the author of *A Guide to Chaucer's Language,* and *Chaucer's Language and the Philosophers' Tradition,* as well as many articles on the English language. He is Associate Editor of the *Year's Work in English Studies* and co-author of its chapter on Chaucer.

THOMAS CABLE is Jane and Roland Blumberg Centennial Professor of English at the University of Texas at Austin and the author of *The Meter and Melody of Beowulf* and many articles on Old and Middle English prosody. He is co-author, with Albert C. Baugh, of *A History of the English Language.*

C. PAUL CHRISTIANSON is Mildred Foss Thompson Professor of English Language and Literature at the College of Wooster, Ohio. His most recent book is *Memorials of the Book Trade in Medieval London: The Archives of Old London Bridge.* In 1983, he was the first recipient of the Frederick R. Goff Fellowship of the Bibliographical Society of America.

JUDITH LAW FISHER is Assistant Professor of English at Trinity University in San Antonio, Texas. She has published in *Victorian Studies* and *Nineteenth-Century Fiction,* and has co-edited and contributed an essay to a collection of essays on nineteenth-century drama, forthcoming from University of Georgia Press. She has also annotated the art criticism of Thackeray as part of a complete edition of annotations to his works, forthcoming from Garland Press.

THOMAS J. HEFFERNAN is Professor of English at the University of Tennessee, Knoxville, and is editor of *Studies in the Age of Chaucer.* He is editing the *Northern Homily Cycle,* on which he has written several articles. He has edited *Popular Literature of Medieval England,* vol. 28 of Tennessee Studies in Literature. His next book, *Sacred Biography,* is forthcoming from Oxford University Press.

MICHAEL MONTGOMERY is Associate Professor of English at the University of South Carolina. He has recently finished an annotated bibliography of Southern American English and has begun research comparing the grammar of Scotch-Irish English to varieties of American English, particularly that found in Southern Appalachia. He is co-author, with John Stratton, of *The Writer's Hotline Handbook* and *The Fast-Track Program for Perfect Spelling* and co-editor, with Guy Bailey, of *Language Variety in the South: Perspectives in Black and White.* He has published a number of articles on Southern American English.

MARY P. RICHARDS is Professor of English and Dean of the College of Liberal Arts at Auburn University as well as Executive Director of the International Society of Anglo-Saxonists. She writes the section, "Manuscripts and Illuminations," for the *Year's Work in Old English Studies* and is the author of a number of articles on manuscripts, law, and literature of the Old English period. Her book, *Texts and Their Traditions in the Medieval Library of Rochester Cathedral Priory,* was published in December, 1988.

JOSEPH B. TRAHERN, JR., is Professor of English at the University of Tennessee, Knoxville, and was Head of the Department from 1978–88. He is the editor of the *Year's Work in Old English Studies* and the author of articles on Old English language and literature. He is currently preparing with John Fisher the *Variorum Chaucer* edition of The Wife of Bath's Prologue and Tale.

Standardizing English was designed by Dariel Mayer, composed by Tseng Information Systems, Inc., and printed and bound by Braun-Brumfield, Inc. The book is set in Times Roman. Text stock is 60-lb. Glatfelter Natural Smooth.